Trade, employment and
industrialisation in Singapore

Trade, employment and industrialisation in Singapore

Linda Lim and Pang Eng Fong

Employment, Adjustment and Industrialisation **2**

INTERNATIONAL LABOUR OFFICE   GENEVA

ISBN 92-2-105231-1
ISSN 0257-3415

First published 1986

ILO publications can be obtained through major booksellers or ILO local offices in many countries, or direct from ILO Publications, International Labour Office, CH-1211 Geneva 22, Switzerland. A catalogue or list of new publications will be sent free of charge from the above address.

Preface

This study on Singapore is one of a number of country studies prepared for the second phase [1] of a research project on employment, trade and North-South co-operation undertaken within the ILO's programme concerning the International Division of Labour. Its authors are Linda Y. Lim and Pang Eng Fong of the National University of Singapore.

The successful economic development of the newly industrialising countries (NICs) is a subject on which a growing amount is being written. This increase reflects the attention that this group of countries is receiving from planners and policy-makers in other developing countries who want to learn how and under which circumstances this success was achieved. It also reflects the concern of policy-makers, entrepreneurs and trade unionists in the countries in which industry had been well established previously about the increased competitiveness of products originating in the NICs and the conditions under which they are being produced.

Some studies on the NICs have examined their economic, industrial and export growth, including the role of foreign capital and multinational enterprises in particular. Others have focused on the extent to which imports from NICs have displaced domestic products in the industrialised countries and the importance of the NICs as markets for them. Still others have dealt with the prevailing conditions of work, including the level of wages and trade union rights.

The studies on the NICs undertaken for our project give due attention to all these factors. Yet their prime focus is on policy. The central question they try to answer is what influence has policy had on their successful growth performance. Such an analysis of policy and its implementation also necessitates an examination of the constraints under which economic policy-makers operate. They include shortages of skilled labour, capital and technology. They are also of an institutional character and determine to a large extent the room for manoeuvre that policy-makers are allowed in the face of the influence and power of the civil service and the social partners, employers and trade unions.

As this study shows, government intervention has been crucial for Singapore's successful development, although it is true that certain initial conditions were also favourable. Upon independence Singapore was not a low-income country by today's standards; it had a well-trained civil service, a well-developed infrastructure and port, an excellent location and, above all, no large agricultural sector to support. The merit of the Government's pragmatic policies is that it has exploited these initial conditions to the full. It used interventionist policies and market signals to accelerate economic growth while at the same time satisfying basic needs and providing a high level of public services. But as the authors say, in so doing "it did not confuse the goal of economic efficiency in production with the goal of equity in distribution".

The Government has become an important force as a generator of savings, and as an intermediary for channelling these savings to investments that it considers important for economic and social reasons. Even more important has been its intervention in wage setting. Through its control over the National Wages Council, yearly wage increases were kept low and behind productivity increases for many years. Even during times of very low unemployment this could be done because of the Government's control over the trade unions and through its immigration policy that allowed more foreigners in whenever the labour market was tight. In more recent years the Government's reluctance for Singapore to become too dependent on foreign workers, as well as a desire to "increase" the skill intensiveness of domestic industry, has led to a series of high annual wage increases.

The impressive way in which the Singapore Government has guided the economy leads one to query whether foreign investment is bound to be accompanied by foreign political influence as some writers maintain. An attractive investment climate gives the country the opportunity to benefit from foreign ideas and technology. Such a climate, say the authors of this study, requires measures to ensure industrial peace and wage stability, but need not compromise a country's economic and political sovereignty. Singapore's recent history seems to prove their case. But is it exceptional? Domestically the Government's strong position owes much to the well-oiled political machinery that serves the party in power and to the strong personality of its Prime Minister who is highly committed to the development of the country and its people.

The economic development of Singapore has brought great gains in welfare to all its citizens in terms of secure jobs, adequate housing, educational opportunities for children and good health facilities. Between 1960 and 1982 their average income increased by almost a factor of 10 in local currency and even more in United States dollars. This is a very impressive record that few (if any) countries can challenge. The Government believes that this record could not or would not have been achieved without a certain degree of control over trade unions, for example, and without limiting the range of personal choices. Choices such as how many children to have, where to live, where to go to school and what to study at school and university have increasingly been influenced by government rules and incentives, but this influence, the authors say, is widely regarded as necessary for social order and progress. Whether to agree with the authors' assessment that the costs of rapid development in Singapore's tightly run society "are minor" remains a question all persons concerned have to answer for themselves.

This study on Singapore is one of a series covering both industrialised and developing countries. They include the Federal Republic of Germany, Japan, the Netherlands, the United Kingdom, the United States, Brazil, Cameroon, the Republic of Korea, the Philippines and Tunisia.

The project was designed by Gijsbert van Liemt of the ILO's Employment and Development Department together with Geoffrey Renshaw of Warwick University and Jacques de Bandt of the University of Paris X, Nanterre. Mr. van Liemt co-ordinated the project throughout.

The entire project was financed by the Government of the Netherlands.

Note

[1] The project is a follow-up of an earlier project carrying the same title. For a description of the results of the first phase, see Geoffrey Renshaw (ed.): *Employment, trade and North-South co-operation* (Geneva, ILO, 1981).

Contents

Chapter 1

Singapore: social and economic characteristics

General country background

The Republic of Singapore is an island nation of 618 square kilometres, situated at the southern end of the busy Straits of Malacca, just north of the equator, in South-East Asia. Its nearest neighbours are the Federation of Malaysia to the north and east, and the Republic of Indonesia to the south and west. About half the total land area of Singapore has been developed for residential, commercial and industrial use. The 1982 population numbered 2.47 million, giving a population density of 3,999 persons per square kilometre. Reflecting its immigrant origins, the population includes 76.7 per cent Chinese, 14.7 per cent Malays, and 6.4 per cent Indians, and is linguistically, culturally and religiously, as well as ethnically, diverse.[1] Though there are four official languages – Malay (the national language), Chinese, Tamil and English – the main language of modern business, government and industry is English.

Founded in 1819 as a British trading post, the colonial city of Singapore grew rapidly to become a major international port. Entrepot trade and British military services formed the basis of its economy. In particular, Singapore served as the port and administrative headquarters for British Malaya. During the Second World War, Malaya was occupied by the Japanese from 1942 to 1945. In 1957, while the rest of Malaya became independent as the Federation of Malaya, Singapore was retained by the British as a separate Crown Colony. Internal self-government was granted in 1959 and 1963 Singapore became independent from the British within the newly established Federation of Malaysia, which included also the former British territories of Sabah and Sarawak in North Borneo.

In August 1965 Singapore separated from the Federation to become a sovereign nation, member of the United Nations and the British Commonwealth of Nations. Since 1959, it has been ruled by the People's Action Party (PAP) under the leadership of Prime Minister Lee Kuan Yew. From 1968 to 1980 the PAP was the only party in parliament, responsible for setting all social and economic policies. (An opposition Member of Parliament was elected in 1981, the first and only one since independence in 1965.) It has engineered an efficient market-based economic system that includes both private and state enterprise.

In international politics, although a member of the non-aligned group of nations, Singapore's leaders generally favour a pro-Western, anti-communist line. In 1967 the country joined with four other like-minded South-East Asian neighbours – Malaysia, Indonesia, Thailand and the Philippines – to form the regional Association of South-East Asian Nations (ASEAN).

Basic economic facts

Despite its tiny land area and small population (it ranks 112th among 125 countries, territories and areas with a population exceeding 1 million), economically Singapore is more than a mini-State. Its 1982 GNP of over US$15,000 million is larger than that of all but three countries in Africa, and exceeds that of much larger and more populous Asian countries like Bangladesh and Burma. In terms of per capita income, Singapore's 1982 level of over US$6,000 in per capita GNP and about US$5,000 in per capita indigenous GNP, ranks it in the top quarter of the world's nations and is comparable to that of European nations such as Spain, Greece, Hungary and Poland.[2] In Asia outside of the Middle East,

Table 1. Basic economic data [1]

	1960 [2]	1970 [2]	1980	1981	1982 [3]
Land area (sq km)	585.1	586.4	617.8	617.9	618.1
Population at mid-year (m)	1.65	2.07	2.41	2.44	2.47
Annual change (%)	2.4	1.5	1.2	1.2	1.2
Labour force (m)	0.48	0.69	1.10	1.15	1.17
Employed (m)	0.45	0.64	1.07	1.11	1.14
Unemployed rate (%)	4.9 [4]	6.0	3.0	2.9	2.6
Gross National Product (GNP) at current market prices (S$m)	2 189.0	5 861.1	23 228.6	27 372.1	30 379.2
Annual change (%)	9.9	14.3	14.0	17.8	11.0
Per capita GNP (S$)	1 329.6	2 825.3	9 622.9	11 202.9	12 290.3
Indigenous GNP (S$m)	n.a.	4 989.9	18 750.5	22 531.6	24 868.6
Per capita indigenous GNP (S$)	n.a.	2 405.4	7 767.7	9 221.8	10 060.9
Annual change (%)	n.a.	11.5	15.8	18.7	9.1
Real per capita indigenous GNP Annual change (%)	n.a.	5.9	7.3	10.5	5.2
Gross Domestic Product (GDP) at 1968 factor cost Annual change (%)	8.7	9.4	10.2	9.9	6.3
Inflation: Annual change (%) Consumer Price Index	1.2	5.6	8.5	8.2	3.9
GDP deflator	1.0	4.9	7.4	6.4	3.8
Gross Domestic Fixed Capital Formation (GDFCF) at 1968 prices Annual change (%)	21.7	10.8	20.1	15.8	24.1
GDFCF as % of GDP	9.4	32.2	41.2	43.8	49.0
Gross National Savings As % of GNP	n.a.	19.3	32.9	35.9	38.5
As % of GDFCF	n.a.	59.8	79.9	81.9	78.7

[1] S$1 = US$0.33 in 1960 and 1970, S$1 = US$0.5 in 1980 and 1982 approximately.   [2] Annual changes refer to averages for the decades 1960-69 and 1970-79 respectively.   [3] Preliminary.   [4] 1957 figure from *Census of Population, 1957.*
Sources: Singapore, Ministry of Trade and Industry: *Economic Survey of Singapore, 1982* (Singapore, Singapore National Printers, 1983); Singapore, Department of Statistics: *Yearbook of Statistics, 1982/83* (Singapore, Singapore National Printers, 1983).

Table 2.   Economic structure: industrial sectors as proportions of Gross Domestic Product, at 1968 market prices (percentages)

Industrial sector	1960	1970	1980	1981	1982 [1]
Agriculture and fishing	3.8	2.3	1.2	1.1	1.0
Quarrying	0.3	0.4	0.3	0.4	0.5
Manufacturing	12.8	20.5	24.1	24.0	21.5
Utilities	2.3	2.6	2.9	2.8	2.7
Construction	3.5	6.3	4.7	5.1	6.5
Trade	31.2	28.1	24.4	23.5	23.2
Transport and communications	13.3	11.3	18.3	19.0	19.5
Financial and business services	7.1	13.9	18.0	19.4	20.7
Other services	17.7	13.6	11.0	10.7	11.1
Total	100.0	100.0	100.0	100.0	100.0
GDP at 1968 prices (S$m)	2 304.5	5 579.3	13 366.5	14 695.2	15 626.9

[1] Preliminary.

Sources: Singapore, Department of Statistics: *Singapore National Accounts 1960-1973* (Singapore, Singapore National Printers, 1975); idem: *Yearbook of Statistics, 1982/83* (Singapore, Singapore National Printers, 1983).

Singapore's per capita income is exceeded only by that of Japan, and the tiny oil-rich newly independent State of Brunei. Its per capita income is comparable to that of Hong Kong, and between two to three times that of newly industrialising countries like the Republic of Korea, Malaysia, Brazil and Mexico.

As the second busiest port in the world, trade and transport and communications have been and still are prominent sectors of the Singapore economy. In 1960 these two sectors, together with other services (then including British military services), accounted for over 60 per cent of total output. Manufacturing ranked fourth in terms of contribution (12.8 per cent) to domestic output. Ten years later it had risen to account for one-fifth of total output, second only to trade. Its GDP contribution reached a peak of 23 per cent in 1981, matching that of trade. Its decline in 1982 reflected the disproportionate impact of the world recession on Singapore's manufacturing exports. In 1982 the transport and communications sector contributed 19.5 per cent to GDP, while the GDP share of the financial and business services sector more than doubled from 7.1 per cent in 1960 to 20.7 per cent in 1982 (see table 2).

Today, in addition to being a major world port and communications centre, Singapore is also an international banking and financial centre, and an important exporter of manufactures from the developing world. Nearly two-thirds of manufacturing output is exported, and manufactures account for 75 per cent of all domestic exports. The openness of the economy is shown by the fact that total trade was three-and-a-half times the value of GNP in 1982, which was the same as in 1960 (see table 3).

Singapore has a small, young and slowly growing population, the result of high rates of population growth in the 1950s (4.4 per cent in the census year of 1957), slowing down to 2.4 per cent per year in the 1960s and 1.5 per cent per year in the 1970s. In 1982 the population growth rate was 1.2 per cent, and nearly

Table 3.   Summary statistics on trade and manufacturing

	1960 [1]	1970 [1]	1980	1981	1982 [2]
Index of industrial production (1978 = 100)	n.a.	43.0	129.2	145.9 [3]	129.6 [3]
Annual change (%)	n.a.	12.1	12.3	5.8 [3]	−11.2 [3]
Manufacturing output as % of GDP at 1968 prices	12.8	20.5	24.1	24.0	21.5
Manufacturing employment as % of total employment	14.3 [4]	22.0	30.1	30.4	29.5
Manufactured direct exports as % of manufacturing output	11.9	59.5	60.6	60.7	60.3
Manufactured direct exports as % of domestic exports	75.5	83.1	77.0	77.7	75.0
Trade/GNP	3.45	2.10	3.99	3.75	3.45
Annual change in total trade (%)	4.2	20.2	34.0	10.5	2.1
Annual change in domestic exports (%)	25.5	26.9	41.8	14.1	−1.0
Balance of payments:					
Current account balance (S$m)	−244.7	−1 750.8	−3 349.3	−2 920.5	−2 737.2
Overall balance (S$m)	140.1	564.8	1 433.8	1 938.4	2 517.5

[1] Annual changes refer to averages for the decades 1960-69 and 1970-79, respectively.   [2] Preliminary.   [3] Fourth quarter figures.   [4] 1957 figure from *Census of Population, 1957.*
Source: Same as table 2.

Table 4.   Singapore: structure of employment by industrial sector (percentages)

Industrial sector	1957	1970	1980	1981	1982
Agriculture and fishing	6.9	3.5	1.6	1.1	1.0
Quarrying	0.3	0.3	0.1	0.1	0.2
Manufacturing	14.3	22.0	30.1	30.4	29.5
Utilities	0.9	1.2	0.8	0.7	0.7
Construction	5.2	6.6	6.7	6.0	6.3
Trade	27.8	23.4	21.3	21.7	22.2
Transport and communications	10.7	12.1	11.1	11.4	11.4
Financial and business services	4.3	4.0	7.4	7.6	7.9
Other services	29.1	26.8	20.9	21.0	20.8
Total	100.0	100.0	100.0	100.0	100.0
Total employment (persons)	471 918	650 892	1 077 090	1 112 818	1 140 507

Sources: Singapore, Department of Statistics: *Report on the Census of Population, 1970* (Singapore, Singapore National Printers, 1973); idem: *Census of Population, 1980*, Release No. 4 (Singapore, Singapore National Printers, 1981); Singapore, Ministry of Labour: *Report on the Labour Force Survey of Singapore, 1981* (Singapore, Printers & Converters, 1982); idem: *Report on the Labour Force Survey of Singapore, 1982* (Singapore, Photoplates Private Ltd., 1983).

half of the population was under the age of 24. The rate of literacy was 85 per cent in 1982, up from 52 per cent in 1957.

Although total population grew by less than half between 1960 and 1982, the labour force more than doubled to 1.17 million in 1982, of whom about one-tenth were non-citizens. Full employment has been maintained since the early 1970s. In 1982, a year of high unemployment in industrial countries, Singapore's unemployment rate was only 2.6 per cent. Manufacturing is today the largest employer in the economy, accounting for 29.5 per cent of total employment, followed by trade with 22.2 per cent, and other services with 20.8 per cent. This pattern of employment contrasts with that found during the census of 1957, when other services (including British military services) employed the most people (29.1 per cent), followed by trade (27.8 per cent), and then by manufacturing (14.3 per cent) (see table 4).

Economic performance, 1960-83

At self-government in 1959, Singapore faced major social and economic problems, namely a stagnant economy, high unemployment, a high rate of population growth, and poor housing conditions. The PAP-led Government quickly embarked on a mass public housing programme, and a vigorous family planning campaign. It also expanded expenditure on education, and instituted industrial development policies to diversify the trade and service-oriented economy. These policies had barely got off the ground when Singapore separated from the Federation of Malaysia in 1965. Its economic vulnerability as a city State with no natural resources was increased by the scheduled withdrawal of British military forces in 1968.

Fortunately, government policies and world economic conditions intervened to produce one of the most spectacularly successful country economic performances in the world. Spurred by a boom in world trade, United States Viet Nam War-induced expenditure in South-East Asia, oil exploration in the region, and a strong take-off into manufacturing for export – all occurring simultaneously in the second half of the 1960s – GNP growth averaged 9.9 per cent annual rate from 1960 until 1969, while real GDP grew at 8.7 per cent a year.

In the 1970s this rapid rate of growth accelerated to an annual average of 14.3 per cent growth in GNP, and 9.4 per cent in real GDP, despite a slowdown in the world economy, the fourfold oil price increase in 1973 and the world recession that followed in 1974 and 1975, and protectionist restrictions in the leading industrialised countries against Singapore's manufactured exports.

In the first two years of the 1980s GDP growth averaged 10 per cent a year, despite the prolonged recession in industrial countries, Singapore's major markets. In 1982 the Singapore economy finally felt the effect of the recession and GDP growth declined to 6.3 per cent. In 1983, with the unexpected strong recovery of the United States economy, its growth quickened to 7.1 per cent, similar to the rate achieved in the two years after the 1974-75 recession.

Since independence in 1965 *economic growth* has derived mainly from the export of goods and services, which accounted for 62 per cent of overall growth between 1965 and 1969, and 63 per cent in the 1970s. In the second half of the 1970s (1975-79), this contribution rose to 70 per cent.[3] Domestic goods exports were concentrated in labour-intensive manufactures such as textiles, clothing, footwear and electronics. The export of services expanded in the 1970s with the growth of the transport and communications sector, especially after 1974. These two sectors were the fastest and third fastest growing sectors of the economy in the 1970s, with manufacturing in second place.

With economic growth came *structural change*: a diversification from trade and services into manufacturing in the 1960s, and a further diversification into transport and communications, and financial and business services in the 1970s, cushioning the economy from the deceleration in the trade and manufacturing sectors in the mid-1970s.

In the 1960s *capital investments* contributed an average of 18 per cent to overall growth, as the physical infrastructure for industrialisation was being built up. This contribution declined to 11 per cent in the 1970s reflecting a drop in private sector investment from 1975 to 1977. In the 1970s, gross national savings financed an average of 60 per cent of domestic investment, rising to an average of nearly 80 per cent for the first three years of the 1980s. Savings rose from an average of 11 per cent of GNP in the 1960s to an average of 19 per cent in the 1970s, and an average of 35 per cent for the period 1980-82.

Economic growth was achieved with relative *price stability* in the 1960s, when the GDP deflator and the consumer price index registered average annual increases of around 1 per cent. In the 1970s world inflation and the oil price crisis added to domestic demand pressures in this extremely open economy, causing the consumer price index to rise by 5.6 per cent a year, and the GDP deflator by 4.9 per cent per year (see table 1). Inflation rates were lower after 1975 than in the early 1970s. They rose in the late 1970s and reached a peak of 8.2 per cent in 1981 before falling rapidly to 1 per cent in 1983 in line with declining world inflation.

Since independence Singapore's overall *balance of payments* each year has been in surplus: the surplus of S$2,500 million in 1982 was 18 times the surplus in 1960. Over the years the current account deficit has widened, reflecting the country's dependence on imports for all its consumption and industrial requirements, and the effect of oil and other commodity price increases. Increased imports of intermediate and capital goods were also needed for the accelerated industrialisation programme – they accounted for over 84 per cent of total retained imports in the 1970s, compared with 66 per cent in the 1960s. The current account deficits were covered by increased net service earnings from the expansion of transport and tourism, averaging S$2,800 million annually in the 1970s compared with S$580 million annually in the 1960s, and by net foreign capital inflows from long-term foreign investments and Singapore's growth as a financial centre. Net capital inflows in the 1970s totalled S$14,300 million, compared with only about S$1,000 million in the 1960s.[4] These inflows continued to increase in the 1980s, averaging S$3,700 million a year for the first three years of the 1980s.[5] Because of healthy balance of payments surpluses and the accumulation of foreign reserves, the Singapore dollar appreciated against most major currencies throughout the 1970s: since the early 1970s it has appreciated by about one-third against the United States dollar.

As the economy thrived, *living standards* improved greatly. Per capita GNP was nine times greater in 1982 than in 1960. Per capita indigenous GNP increased four times between 1970 and 1982, and registered an average annual growth rate of 5.9 per cent in real terms during the 1970s (see table 1). Rapid growth apparently has not worsened the distribution of income, at least until the mid-1970s.[6] *Employment* more than doubled between 1960 and 1982. Full employment was first reached in the early 1970s, and maintained since the late 1970s. In fact, since the early 1970s labour shortages have been persistent in many fast-growing sectors of the economy. To sustain its high rate of economic growth, Singapore has had to import both professional and unskilled foreign workers.

Manufacturing performance

Since 1960, with the exception of the 1974-75 and 1982-83 recession periods, manufacturing has been the fastest-growing sector of the economy, with annual rates of output growth averaging between 20 and 25 per cent. It ranks only slightly behind trade as the largest sector of the economy (see table 2), and employs more people than any other sector (30 per cent of the total). Manufactured exports have grown more rapidly, and manufacturing employment more slowly, than manufacturing output. Manufactured exports account for three-fifths of all manufacturing output, and for 75 per cent of total domestic exports (see table 3).

Within the manufacturing sector, there has been a change in the industrial composition of production (see table 5). In 1960 nearly 90 per cent of all manufacturing was for the domestic market and food and printing were the largest industries. Two decades later 60 per cent of manufacturing output was exported, and petroleum, transport equipment and electrical machines were the major industries. These three industries together accounted for 60 per cent of all manufacturing value-added in 1982.

Table 5.   Singapore: percentage distribution of manufacturing value-added by industry

Industry	1960	1970	1980	1981	1982 [1]
Food	31	12	5	6	6
Printing	17	— [2]	4 [3]	5 [3]	5 [3]
Metal	8	7	2	2	2
Wood	7	6	2	2	2
Transport equipment	2	15	12	12	11
Electrical and electronics	6	12	33	32	31
Petroleum	— [2]	19	17	17	18
Chemicals	— [2]	— [2]	5	5	5
Others	25	29	20	19	20
Total	100	100	100	100	100

[1] Preliminary.   [2] Included in "Others" category.   [3] Includes paper products.

Sources: Singapore, Ministry of Trade and Industry: *Economic Survey of Singapore, 1979* (Singapore, Singapore National Printers, 1980), p. 65; idem: *Economic Survey of Singapore, 1981* (Singapore, Singapore National Printers, 1981), p. 83; idem: *Economic Survey of Singapore, 1982* (Singapore, Singapore National Printers, 1983), pp. 100-101.

Industrial growth in the 1960s and early 1970s was concentrated mainly in labour-intensive industries such as textiles, garments, food, paper and wood products. Since the mid-1970s manufacturing growth has been concentrated in higher value-added industries, namely petroleum refining, electrical and electronic machinery, shipbuilding and oil rig construction, metal engineering and precision equipment, and chemicals. Except for petroleum and chemicals, these industries employ large numbers of unskilled workers, but they have all been upgrading themselves in response to labour shortages and competitive pressures.

Concerned about Singapore's potential declining international competitiveness in labour-intensive manufactured exports, and the ever-present threat of protectionism in developed country markets, the Government in 1979 announced the launching of a "Second Industrial Revolution". It has introduced policies to encourage the upgrading of established industries and the establishment of new ones which are more capital- than labour-intensive and employ high technology and skills to make high-value products for export. The designated "priority industries" for the 1980s include chemical process industries, metal engineering and machinery, heavy engineering industries, and the electrical and electronics industries. Investments in these industries have grown rapidly since 1980 and have strengthened the growth potential of the manufacturing sector.

The institutional environment

Government

The State is the major actor in the institutional environment surrounding the Singapore economy. (Its role will be discussed in greater detail in Chapter 3.) The ruling party, in power since 1959, wields complete political control, through its nearly exclusive representation in parliament, and its control of the civil service, the labour movement (through the National Trades Union Congress) and local community organisations (including the People's Association).[7] Development strategy and social and economic policy are decided by the Government, and implemented in limited consultation with workers' and employers' and other citizens' groups. Within the Government itself, policy measures are typically initiated by the top political leaders and the civil service rather than by parliament. Decision-making in the society is thus highly centralised.

In general, the Government subscribes to a philosophy of economic liberalism, with some state controls. Given the openness of the economy, market forces, especially world market forces, are the dominant influence on resource allocation, especially in the large external sector. There are no foreign exchange controls. In the financial market exchange rates and interest rates are determined largely by market forces. Since Singapore is a free port, there are few import tariffs, mostly to raise revenue and to curb consumption of certain "luxury" items, such as alcohol, tobacco and motor vehicles. Protective tariffs on local industry have been gradually removed, and are now levied at a low rate on a few items such as textiles, garments and footwear. Domestic price controls apply only to a few items including sugar and cement.

Apart from minor health, safety and pollution regulations, and regulations on the employment of labour and industrial relations, there are virtually no controls on private enterprise and investment. There are no anti-monopoly laws, no approval or licensing process for foreign or local private investments, no technology transfer controls or required registration of contracts or licences, no import controls or required domestic value-added proportions, and no limitations on profit remittances, technology payments or capital repatriation overseas. The Government does, however, influence the sectoral allocation of resources, through its various investment incentive schemes granting tax exemptions, write-offs and other subsidies and allowances to desired investments. Investments, especially in the manufacturing sector, are also affected by international policies, such as the external protection offered to manufactured exports by the Generalised System of Preferences (GSP) and the Multi-Fibre Arrangement (MFA).

Despite the relative lack of controls, and the dominance of market forces in allocating resources, Singapore's domestic economy is far from a laissez-faire one. The Government's post-independence development strategy to diversify the economy and to promote manufacturing for export has been based on encouraging private investment, including foreign private investment, by providing tax incentives in an economy with free trade and capital flows, and excellent infrastructure. Government statutory boards, state enterprises and joint ventures provide all social and economic infrastructural facilities, and the basic needs of the majority of the population. They also engage directly in productive activities, often in competition with the private sector.

The Public Utilities Board (PUB), Telecommunications Authority of Singapore (TAS) and Jurong Town Corporation (JTC) are state monopolies providing utilities, communications services, and industrial estates, respectively. The Housing Development Board (HDB) builds and manages apartment blocks and industrial estates. Over 70 per cent of Singapore's total population today live in HDB flats. The Urban Redevelopment Authority (URA) engages in urban renewal and property development. The Economic Development Board (EDB) promotes local and foreign investments and approves incentives for manufacturers. The Singapore Tourist Promotion Board (STPB) promotes tourism and develops tourist facilities and services.

In the social services area, the Ministry of Health provides public health care and medical services. The Ministry of Education is in charge of education for the mass of the population from primary to tertiary level. The Vocational and Industrial Training Board (VITB) offers vocational and industrial training opportunities to secondary-school leavers and the Ministry of Environment provides sanitation services, and parks and recreational services. The Singapore Broadcasting Corporation (SBC) is responsible for state radio and television.

There is a state airline, Singapore Airlines (SIA), a state trading company (INTRACO), a state industrial research institute, the Singapore Institute of Standards and Industrial Research (SISIR), a state shipping company, Neptune Orient Lines (NOL), two state-joint venture shipyards, Keppel and Sembawang

Shipyards. In addition, the Government through its two holding companies (Temasek and Shengli) has invested in productive and profit-making enterprises including an arms-making factory, farms and zoological gardens.

In the financial sector the Central Provident Fund (CPF) and Post Office Savings Bank (POSB) hold a majority of national savings. The Monetary Authority of Singapore (MAS) acts as a central bank and is responsible for monetary policy. The newly incorporated Government of Singapore Investment Corporation (GOSIC) manages foreign exchange resources. The Development Bank of Singapore (DBS), a publicly quoted company with majority government share, operates as a commercial bank and invests in many private enterprises.

Thus, unlike governments in predominantly laissez-faire economies, the Singapore Government does more than provide infrastructure and social services. On its own, or in partnership with private enterprises or shareholders, it also finances and engages in direct production. Many state and quasi-state institutions, including those providing infrastructure and social services, are managed as profit-seeking enterprises, reflecting a government philosophy opposed to subsidies and in favour of profit-making.

Because of its heavy direct and indirect involvement in the economy, the State can exercise considerable leverage on the domestic macro-economy, beyond the use of conventional public revenue and expenditure instruments. More than half of domestic income passes through government hands in one way or another – through the 46 per cent share of earned income which goes to the CPF in compulsory employer and employee contributions, the 2 per cent payroll tax and 4 per cent Skills Development Fund (SDF) levy on wages, personal and corporate income taxes, indirect taxes, and the tariffs charged and incomes earned by the various statutory boards and state enterprises. The Government is also the largest employer in the economy, accounting for 10 per cent of total employment. It regulates wage increases through the National Wage Council (NWC), and influences the construction sector through its own property development activities and controls on private sector construction. It also regulates, through the Monetary Authority of Singapore, financial markets and the domestic money supply.

Despite these powers, the Government has rarely chosen to regulate the macro-economy in the typical Keynesian counter-cyclical manner. Exceptions are pump priming through government investment in 1974-75 and 1982-83 to counter the effects of world recession, and the maintenance of lower-than-world inflation rates throughout the 1970s by restraining wage increases and siphoning off increasing proportions of purchasing power through CPF contributions. The construction of a mass rapid transit system begun in 1983 will have a stimulative effect on the economy and offset to some extent the expected decline in other building activities in the mid- and late-1980s. In general, however, state economic controls and incentives are more often used to effect micro-economic changes, such as labour market adjustments and the sectoral allocation of resources than as counter-cyclical tools.

Labour

From the 1950s until the early 1960s, Singapore was characterised by a politically active and radical, confrontationist labour movement with left-wing leadership. The PAP came to power in 1959 as the moderate wing of a coalition based on the grass-roots support of this labour movement, but quickly achieved dominance by suppressing the left-wing within and without its own ranks. In particular, left-wing unions were deregistered and their leaders and sympathetic politicians arrested and placed under political detention without trial in 1963. The PAP-supported National Trades Union Congress (NTUC) became the national umbrella organisation of a newly pacified and moderate labour movement.

After Singapore's separation from Malaysia in 1965, the Government's strategy of industrial development and employment generation hinged on attracting foreign investment in labour-intensive, export-oriented manufacturing. This, it believed, required low wages and labour discipline, which were ensured by administrative regulations governing the registration and deregistration of unions, compulsory arbitration procedures to limit strikes, and new labour laws in 1968. The Employment Act standardised terms and conditions of employment, defining the maximum and minimum limits of fringe benefits. The Industrial Relations Amendment Act removed such issues as recruitment, retrenchment, dismissal, etc., from collective negotiations and defined the framework and procedures for labour negotiation and conflict resolution.[8]

These political and legal moves achieved their aims. They de-politicised the labour movement, established *de facto* government control over unions, transferred bargaining power from workers to employers, and ushered in an era of labour peace that persists to this day. Since 1968, man-days lost through strikes and other labour action have been negligible. Since 1978 there have been no industrial stoppages. The industrial relations system is one of tripartism based on co-operation rather than confrontation among workers, employers and Government. Union membership reached a peak of nearly 250,000 or about a quarter of the workforce in 1979. Since 1979 it has fallen, despite employment growth in all sectors. More than 90 per cent of total union membership is affiliated with the NTUC, which has itself become involved in many co-operative ventures, including profit-making consumer enterprises such as supermarkets, taxis, insurance, workers' education and welfare programmes including child-care centres.

In 1972 the tripartite National Wages Council (NWC) was formed with representatives from the Government, the NTUC and employers' associations. Its main function so far has been to formulate annual wage guide-lines for the economy. Until 1979 annual wage increases were modest, less than 10 per cent a year in nominal terms, with the exception of a large 20 per cent increase in 1974 to compensate for the previous year's high inflation and declining real wages. In 1979, as part of the restructuring strategy, the Government through the mechanism of the NWC introduced a three-year "corrective" wage policy to "restore wages to market levels". Labour costs increased by an average of 20 per cent a year in the first two years of this policy, and 28 per cent in the third year. In 1982 and 1983 nominal wage increases returned to the pre-1979 level of 7-8 per cent a year.

Since the first appearance of full employment in the early 1970s the Singapore economy has increasingly relied on the importation of unskilled and skilled foreign labour to make up the shortfall in the domestic labour supply. Import of skilled labour and expatriate personnel in the higher-income levels has generally been liberal, and that of unskilled labour has also been liberal, until recently. In 1980 one in nine workers in the labour force was foreign, a proportion which the Government plans to reduce by phasing out unskilled foreign labour by 1992.[9]

Foreign enterprises

Foreign enterprises have played a major role in the Singapore economy since colonial days. Originally concentrated in the trade and services sectors, foreign enterprises have since 1960 greatly increased their role in manufacturing. Singapore's industrialisation programme, indeed its whole development strategy, relies heavily on foreign investment, technology, and expertise. Foreign enterprises are welcomed and encouraged with a host of investment incentives, and there are liberal policies regarding the employment of expatriate personnel and professionals.

Although the contribution of foreign capital to capital formation fell from 70 per cent in the early 1960s to around 30 per cent in the late 1970s, foreign capital inflow in absolute terms increased from S$1,100 million in 1970 to S$2,700 million in 1982.[10] In the manufacturing sector the share of foreign investment in gross fixed assets has risen from 45 per cent in 1966 to 81 per cent in 1979. In 1979 two-thirds of gross capital formation in manufacturing were in enterprises with some foreign capital, of which four-fifths was in wholly or majority-foreign owned enterprises (accounting for 54 per cent of total gross capital formation in manufacturing).[11] In 1982 over two-thirds of the net investment commitments of S$1,700 million in manufacturing were from foreign countries.[12] As shown in table 6, foreign manufacturing investments in terms of gross fixed assets are largest in the petroleum industry, followed by the electrical and electronics industries, metal and engineering industries, and chemicals industry respectively. These four industries together accounted for three-quarters of all foreign manufacturing assets in Singapore in 1981. Compared with 1970, the shares of petroleum and chemicals have dropped, while those of the other key industries have increased. In terms of net investment commitments in 1982 the three leading industries – respectively, electrical and electronics, metal and engineering, and petroleum – together accounted for about two-thirds of the S$1,700 million committed.

Table 7 shows the distribution of manufacturing foreign investment by region of origin. In terms of gross fixed assets in 1981 Europe is the leader, followed by North America, and then by other parts of Asia. The large share of European countries reflects their huge investments in the petroleum industry (Royal Dutch Shell, British Petroleum, etc.). In terms of net investment commitments, the Europeans lag behind other Asian investors (including those from

Table 6. Singapore: investments by industry

Industry	Gross fixed assets (%)			Net investment commitments (%)		
	1970	1979	1981	1980	1981	1982
Petroleum	55.8	41.4	40.3	14.0	8.4	22.2
Metal and engineering	5.3	11.2	12.6	13.8	22.1	18.3
Transport equipment	5.1	6.1	4.9	4.1	13.9	4.0
Electrical and electronics	8.2	14.8	17.3	28.1	23.4	21.0
Chemicals	6.1	3.9	5.1	12.5	8.3	3.7
Others	19.5	22.6	19.8	27.5	23.9	30.8
Total	100.0 = S$995 m	100.0 = S$6 349 m	100.0 = S$8 650 m	100.0 = S$1 426 m	100.0 = S$1 929 m	100.0 = S$1 747 m

Sources: Singapore, Economic Development Board: *Annual Report 1979/80*; idem: *Annual Report 1981/82*; Singapore, Ministry of Trade and Industry: *Economic Survey of Singapore, 1980* (Singapore, Singapore National Printers, 1981), p. 84; idem: *Economic Survey of Singapore, 1982* (Singapore, Singapore National Printers, 1983). p. 102.

Table 7. Singapore: foreign investment in manufacturing by region of origin

Region	Gross fixed assets (%)			Net investment commitments (%)		
	1971	1979	1981	1972	1979	1981
North America	32.1	29.0	31.1	12.7	27.6	34.9
Europe	40.7	38.3	38.8	11.1	17.5	13.6
Asia	27.2	32.6	30.1	56.6	42.1	20.0
Total foreign				80.4	87.2	68.5
Total local				19.6	12.8	31.5
Total foreign and local	100.0 = $1 575 m	100.0 = $6 349 m	100.0 = $8 650 m	100.0 = $195 m	100.0 = $943 m	100.0 = $1 938 m

Sources: Singapore, Economic Development Board: *Annual Report 1979/80*; idem: *Annual Report 1981/82*.

Japan and Hong Kong) and investors from North America. North American investors contributed the largest share (34.9 per cent) of new investments in 1981. Compared with investors from other regions, their relative position has increased the most since 1972.

Despite their dominance of the industrial sector, and strong representation in other sectors of the economy, foreign-owned enterprises do not have a strong say in economic policy-making. Like other economic actors in the system – local enterprises and workers – they essentially respond to government policy initiatives. Both local and foreign employers' associations – like the Singapore National Employers' Federation, the Singapore Chinese Chamber of Commerce, the Singapore Manufacturers' Association, the American Business Council and other nationality groupings – are only indirectly involved in making economic policy. Employer groups are represented in various tripartite bodies including the tripartite National Wages Council, the Economic Development Board, the National Productivity Council, Jurong Town Corporation and other statutory bodies. Though they play only a minor role in economic policy formulation, foreign firms are crucial to the success of such policy, given their weight in the economy as a whole. For this reason, the Government pays close attention to the views and reactions of foreign firms to its development policies.

Appraisal

At the time of self-government in 1959 the Singapore economy faced serious problems of economic stagnation and rising unemployment. The Government's strategy for development then was focused on industrialisation, particularly import-substituting industrialisation for the enlarged national market of the Federation of Malaysia, which Singapore joined in 1963. Separation from Malaysia in 1965 forced Singapore to change its industrial development strategy. Given its very small domestic market and high unemployment, the strategy chosen was that of labour-intensive manufacturing for export, led by multinational corporations from the Western nations and, later, Japan.

This strategy has been spectacularly successful in establishing a manufacturing base in the country, in absorbing labour, and contributing to Singapore's rapid economic growth and rise in real incomes since 1965. This growth has also been boosted by world trade expansion in the late 1960s and early 1970s, and by Singapore's increasing importance not only as a world port and communications centre, but also as a regional and international financial and business services centre. Liberal government economic policies together with political stability and fortuitous domestic, regional and world economic circumstances created a favourable environment for rapid economic growth.

Even before the world recession of 1974-75 the rapidly expanding Singapore economy was beginning to face new challenges. These include domestic labour shortages, declining competitiveness in export manufacturing, and a narrow manufacturing base. In 1979 the Government announced a strategy of accelerated industrial restructuring – the strategy was in fact initiated in the early

1970s, but was set aside in the wake of the oil shock and world recession of the mid-1970s. This strategy focuses on upgrading technology and skills to export more capital-intensive, high-value manufactured products, and phasing out low-value, labour-intensive activities. As in the past, foreign enterprises are expected to take the lead in this "Second Industrial Revolution", while domestic policy concentrates on increasing labour productivity.

Government policy-makers have correctly perceived the problem of Singapore's continued viability as an exporter of manufactured products and have proposed the remedy of upgrading manufacturing activities. Given Singapore's small size, its short industrial history, lack of skills and manpower, and the competitiveness of markets for high-technology products, which other newly industrialising countries are trying to penetrate, the long-term prospects for this necessary strategy appear uncertain. In the last few years the strategy seems to have worked as foreign investors upgraded in response to market pressures and government incentives. Manufacturing, after an absolute decline in 1982, rebounded in 1983 partly because of new industries (e.g. computer peripherals) established since 1980, and partly because older labour-intensive industries like garments and consumer electronics have been surprisingly strong. In the longer term it is likely that the small size and flexibility of the Singapore economy will enable it to occupy intermediate niches in high-technology industries. But Singapore's dependence on foreign enterprise, technology, skills and labour is also likely to grow.

Unlike the situation at independence in 1965 when Singapore had no alternative but to turn to foreign-led labour-intensive manufacturing for export, Singapore today has more alternatives. It can capitalise on its location, excellent infrastructure and human skills to promote the export of services, including industrial and computer services, to the region and the world. By promoting services with appropriate incentives and legislation, Singapore may be able to transcend its binding domestic resource constraints and develop in the long term an even more resilient economy than it has now.

Notes

[1] Singapore, Department of Statistics: *Yearbook of Singapore, 1982/83* (Singapore, Singapore National Printers, 1982).

[2] World Bank: *World Development Report, 1983* (Oxford University Press for the World Bank, 1983), table 1.

[3] Singapore, Ministry of Trade and Industry: *Economic Survey of Singapore, 1979* (Singapore, Singapore National Printers, 1980), p. 61.

[4] ibid., p. 63.

[5] Singapore, Department of Statistics: *Yearbook of Statistics, 1982-83* (Singapore, Singapore National Printers, 1983), p. 85.

[6] See Pang Eng Fong: "Growth, inequality and race in Singapore", in *International Labour Review* (Geneva, ILO), Jan. 1975, pp. 15-28; Bhanoji Rao and M. K. Ramakrishnan: *Income inequality in Singapore* (Singapore, Singapore University Press, 1981); Department of Statistics: *Report on the household expenditure survey, 1977/1978* (Singapore, Singapore National Printers, 1979).

[7] For an analysis of Singapore's political system, see Chan Heng Chee: *The dynamics of one party dominance: The PAP at the grassroots* (Singapore, Singapore University Press, 1976).

[8] For an analysis of the evolution of Singapore's industrial relations system, see Pang Eng Fong: "Singapore", in Albert A. Blum (ed.): *International handbook of industrial relations: Contemporary developments and research* (Westport, Connecticut, Greenwood Press, 1981), pp. 481-497.

[9] For a discussion of foreign labour in Singapore, see Pang Eng Fong and Linda Lim: "Foreign labor and economic development in Singapore", in *International Migration Review*, Fall 1982, Vol. 16, No. 3, pp. 548-576.

[10] Singapore, Ministry of Trade and Industry: *Economic Survey of Singapore, 1982* (Singapore, Singapore National Printers, 1983).

[11] Pang Eng Fong: *Foreign indirect investment in Singapore: A preliminary report*, paper prepared for the OECD Development Centre, February 1981, Appendix tables I and II.

[12] Singapore, Economic Development Board: *Annual Report, 1981-1982*.

Chapter 2

Economic development of Singapore

Development objectives, plans and strategy

Since the attainment of internal self-government in 1959 Singapore's Government has designed the country's economic development strategy. A First Development Plan was instituted for 1960-64, but since independence in 1965 there have been no formal five-year plans. Development policies and public expenditure programmes are introduced in annual government budgets, and in ad hoc measures throughout the year. Only for the 1980s has a longer-term indicative plan – the Ten-Year Plan [1] – been issued.

The main aim of the First Development Plan was to diversify the entrepot- and service-based economy, by encouraging import-substituting industrialisation for the anticipated Malaysian Common Market. Singapore expected to become the manufacturing as well as trade and services centre of the Federation of Malaysia which it joined in 1963.

With separation from Malaysia in 1965, these hopes were dashed. Singapore's domestic market was too small to support import-substituting industrialisation, and the Government's development strategy turned towards export manufacturing instead. But because the main objective was employment creation through industrialisation, all labour-intensive manufacturing was encouraged. Tariff protection was retained or granted to several industries which were, however, expected to develop export markets as well as supply local demand – as textiles, garments, footwear and television assembly did. Export manufacturing was led by subsidiaries of offshore sourcing multinationals, especially in the electronics industry.

This strategy of labour-intensive manufacturing, especially but not exclusively for export, continued from 1966 to 1973, by which time full employment and emerging domestic labour shortages had led to plans for industrial upgrading into less labour-intensive activities. The onset of the severe 1974-75 world recession, which particularly affected labour-intensive export industries, delayed this intended restructuring. No new industrial policies were introduced during the market-led post-recession recovery from 1976-78.

In 1979 the Government launched what was termed a "Second Industrial Revolution" to restructure the economy into one based on high-value activities. The rationale for this strategy is detailed in Singapore's indicative development plan for the 1980s, which sets a GDP growth target of 8-10 per cent a year, and identifies manufacturing, trade, tourism, transport and communication, and "brain" services (including financial, medical and architectural services) as the five pillars of growth.[2] Both internal and external factors prompted the restructuring strategy. Internally, the economy was experiencing widespread labour shortages which were likely to become more severe because of the absolutely diminishing pool of new labour force entrants. Politically, a strategy of relying on labour-intensive activities could not satisfy the rising expectations of workers for better pay which was only possible with the creation of more skilled jobs. Externally, Singapore was beginning to lose its competitive advantage in producing labour-intensive manufactures to other developing countries, and faced the ever-present threat of protectionism in developed country markets. Moreover, the industrial countries were likely to continue growing slowly in the 1980s and Singapore had to find new markets for its exports.

To encourage firms to upgrade and mechanise, the Government adopted three sets of policies, of which only one is really new in the history of industrial development in Singapore. These policies are a wage correction policy designed to raise labour costs to promote efficient use of scarce labour, additional investment incentives for desired industries, and expansion of training and educational facilities for new labour force entrants and workers in industry.

Wage correction policy

Prior to 1972 market forces determined wages in Singapore. To ensure orderly wage changes the Government set up in 1972 a tripartite National Wages Council. Since then, wage guide-lines, though voluntary, have strongly influenced wage increases in both the private and public sectors. During and in the few years immediately after the world recession of the mid-1970s, the Council recommended modest wage increases to ensure the competitiveness of the labour-intensive export industries. These guide-lines, while helping to keep exports competitive, did not encourage firms to use labour efficiently or to upgrade their operations quickly. As a result, labour shortages intensified and manufacturing productivity suffered, growing by an average of only 2-3 per cent a year until 1979. In 1979 the Council began a three-year wage correction policy, i.e. recommended high wage bill increases averaging nearly 20 per cent a year, to restore wages to market levels. Workers, however, enjoyed average wage increases of about 14 per cent a year because part of the increase in employer wage bills was channelled into increased Central Provident Fund contributions and into a Skills Development Fund to train and upgrade workers affected by the restructuring strategy. Thus the inflationary consequences of the wage correction policy were minimised. In 1980 the Council introduced the idea of a second-tier payment to reward above-average workers. Because of implementation problems, this idea did not find much favour with employers who dropped it the following year. The Government has indicated that in future wage changes will be closely tied to productivity gains. The Council's guide-lines will be more flexible to reflect, more fully than in the past, the diversity of productivity gains among firms.

The wage correction policy has apparently met with some success. Employment creation in the economy, especially in the manufacturing sector, has slowed down. National productivity gains doubled to about 5 per cent a year in

1980-81 before slipping to 2 per cent in 1982 largely because of weakening external demand for Singapore's manufacturing exports. In 1983, in line with improved economic performance, productivity growth rose again to nearly 4 per cent. Foreign investment commitments, most of it in desired industries, rose to an all-time record of S$1,900 million in 1981, despite the large wage increases. In 1982 and 1983 external confidence in the Singapore economy remained high and foreign investments have continued to flow into Singapore. At the same time, there has been a resurgence of local manufacturing investment commitments; local investors in 1982 accounted for a third of all new investment commitments in manufacturing compared to an annual average of less than a fifth before 1979.

Industrial investment incentives

To stimulate investment in desired high-value activities, the Government has modified old fiscal incentives and introduced new ones.[3] The basic tax incentive was, and still is, pioneer status which exempts from tax company profits for a period of five to ten years, depending on such factors as the level of investment, its capital and skill intensity, research and development spending, and so on. Pioneer status can be granted to deserving projects even if the investment is less than S$1 million. The period of exemption from company tax can be longer than ten years for projects involving advanced technology and long gestation periods.

A second important incentive, first introduced in 1967 and liberalised since then, encourages exports by taxing approved export profits at 4 per cent rather than at the usual rate of 40 per cent. The normal incentive period is five years, but it can be as long as 15 years for projects with fixed capital expenditure of over S$150 million, provided Singapore permanent residents own at least 50 per cent of the paid-up capital.

Firms that do not qualify for pioneer status or export incentives can obtain an investment allowance which allows an approved manufacturing or technical servicing project a tax credit of up to 50 per cent of new fixed investment in plant, machinery, and factory buildings. The credit can be set off against the profits of the company for the year in which the capital spending takes place.

In addition to the pioneer status, export incentive and investment allowance schemes, the Government has a variety of other incentives to encourage plant expansion, automation, computerisation, and R & D spending. Capital equipment can be completely written off in five to ten years, plant and machinery for R & D can be completely depreciated in three years, and purchase of computers in one year. Double deduction of R & D spending is permitted, lump-sum payments for manufacturing licenses can be capitalised and written off in five years, and an investment allowance of up to 50 per cent of the capital investment in research and development is available.

A capital assistance scheme was set up in 1975 with a budget of S$100 million to provide equity and/or loan capital to industrial investors with specialised projects that will benefit Singapore economically and technologically. Over two-thirds of the budget has so far been disbursed. The Economic Development Board, which administers the scheme, also has a small industries finance scheme to help small firms to upgrade their operations and diversify their product lines. Local firms are also eligible for small development grants under a product development scheme, another scheme administered by the Board.

In legislation, all the incentive schemes except those aimed specifically at small or local firms are available to both local and foreign enterprises. In practice, however, foreign enterprises which dominate the manufacturing sector in terms of value-added and exports have benefited more than local firms because of their larger investments and higher technology levels.

Compared with the 1960s and 1970s investment incentives are now more selectively awarded. Favoured projects are those that are technologically sophisticated and also capital- and skill-intensive. The Economic Development Board has drawn up a list of industries for priority development. The list includes industries making such products as computers, instrumentation and industrial controls, telecommunication equipment, advanced electronic components, solar cells and optical fibres, precision machine tools, photographic and optical instruments, medical instruments and devices, office equipment, industrial machinery including robotics, oilfield equipment, aircraft components, automotive components, ship machinery, diesel engines, mining equipment, speciality industrial chemicals, pharmaceuticals and engineering plastics.[4]

Besides planning to attract investment in priority industries to broaden Singapore's industrial base, the Government is encouraging local manufacturers who cannot pay market wages to relocate to other countries. The relocation of such firms, it believes, will not only help neighbouring economies but also give industries in Singapore ready access to key inputs. It will also encourage with loans and incentives the expansion of supporting industries to link up with high value-added industries. In short, the Singapore Government is clear about the industries it wants and the adjustment that both local and foreign firms must make to remain viable in Singapore in the future.

Expansion of training and educational facilities

A third vital component of the restructuring strategy is the accelerated expansion of educational and training opportunities not only for new labour force entrants but also for workers already in industry. With the emphasis on skill and technology upgrading, post-secondary technical and professional training has become a high priority of government policy. Since 1979 the National University of Singapore has increased rapidly enrolments in its professional faculties, particularly engineering. A new Nanyang Technological Institute opened in 1982 to train practically oriented engineers for industry. The Singapore Polytechnic, Ngee Ann Polytechnic and the Vocational and Industrial Training Board which train technicians and skilled workers for industry will greatly increase their enrolments in the 1980s.

Government planners project that the various formal post-secondary institutions will need to enrol over 30,000 students each year during the 1980s if the high growth targets for manufacturing and the economy are to be met. This number exceeds the available pool of qualified Singaporean school-leavers, who are already in short supply relative to the number of available training places. To meet intake targets, the Government will admit increasingly large numbers of foreign students, mostly Malaysians, who in return for tuition and scholarship awards have to work in Singapore or for Singapore companies for varying periods of time after their graduation. There are no formal agreements between the Singapore and Malaysian Governments obligating Malaysian students to work in Singapore or for Singapore firms to hire them after their studies.

In addition to the formal post-secondary institutions, the Government has developed, in some cases jointly with multinational firms or with the support of industrial countries, many practically oriented industrial training institutes. The Economic Development Board runs four Joint Industry Training Centres, three of them operated jointly with international companies (Philips, Tata, and Brown-Boveri) and the fourth with the Japanese Government. Besides the four training centres which impart general skills, the Board has in co-operation with three foreign governments set up three institutes of technology to provide more specialised training in fields such as tool and die design, production processes, robotics, microprocessor and computer applications, and computer software technology. The three institutes are the German Singapore Institute of Production Technology (established in 1982), the Japanese Singapore Institute of Software Technology (1982) and the French Singapore Institute of Electrotechnology (1983).

Apart from expanding training institutions that prepare new entrants for the job market, the Government is actively encouraging the expansion of training opportunities for workers already in industry, especially the half a million workers with little or no education. It has developed a Basic Education for Skills Training (BEST) programme to upgrade the literacy, numeracy, and English-language skills of workers with little formal schooling. Started in 1982, the programme had an enrolment of 22,000 in 1983 and is expected to enrol 40,000 workers a year from 1984.

In 1979, as part of its restructuring strategy, the Government set up a Skills Development Fund to upgrade skills and retrain workers who might be made redundant by the restructuring strategy. Firms have to pay 4 per cent of the wages of their employees earning less than S$750 a month to the Fund, but they can apply for grants to cover as much as 90 per cent of approved training costs. Since 1979, as collections by the Fund accumulate, the objectives of the Fund have been widened to include grants to help firms mechanise and automate their operations. At the end of October 1983 the Fund had committed S$153 million in training grants to nearly 17,000 successful applications to train over 136,000 workers or 12 per cent of the workforce.

Government training and educational programmes are not restricted to Singaporeans only. Because of the declining number of qualified Singaporeans the Government has increased the intake of foreign students into post-secondary and tertiary institutions. At the same time, it is encouraging foreign skilled and professional workers to settle in Singapore, and encouraging highly educated women to marry and have more than two children. It has also instituted policies such as flexible working hours, part-day work, etc., to induce more women to join the workforce. The long-term aim is to expand the locally available supply of skills needed for a modern industrial economy, and not to become dependent on unskilled foreign labour. High dependence on unskilled foreign workers, the Government believes, not only retards industrial restructuring but also creates problems of integration, especially if the foreign labour is imported from countries whose populations have different social and cultural characteristics from that of Singapore.

The development experience

Since the late 1960s Singapore has been one of the world's fastest growing economies. As table 8 shows, real GDP grew at an average rate of 9.5 per cent between 1960 and 1982, with the fastest increase occurring between 1966 and 1970 (16.1 per cent a year), when there was a spurt of both private and public sector investment, the former occurring mostly in export-oriented manufacturing industries. The manufacturing sector experienced a real rate of growth over the period (12 per cent), the third fastest-growing sector after the financial and business services sector (14.6 per cent) and construction (12.3 per cent). Other sectors which experienced above average growth rates were transport and communications (11.1 per cent) and utilities (9.9 per cent), while the two largest sectors in 1960, trade and other services, experienced slower growth (7.7 per cent and 6 per cent respectively). This differential growth accounts for the structural shift of the economy from entrepot and service activities to a manufacturing and financial centre.

Table 8. Rate of growth of GDP by industrial sector 1960-82 (at constant 1968 prices) (percentages)

Industrial sector	1960-65	1966-70	1960-70	1971-75	1976-82 [1]	1971-82 [1]	1960-82 [1]
Total	5.5	16.1	10.1	8.8	8.7	8.6	9.5
Agriculture and fishing	1.1	4.5	4.0	−0.6	0.6	1.0	2.8
Quarrying	4.4	14.7	10.0	14.5	9.3	11.2	10.9
Manufacturing	9.1	23.4	15.1	8.5	8.3	8.6	12.0
Utilities	5.1	15.0	10.6	8.7	9.6	9.2	9.9
Construction	19.1	17.2	16.1	7.0	9.4	8.7	12.3
Trade	2.8	13.5	8.2	8.3	6.8	7.0	7.7
Transport and communications	1.6	16.6	7.8	14.3	13.8	14.0	11.1
Financial and business services	10.5	29.4	17.0	11.3	12.8	12.4	14.6
Other services	5.3	8.4	6.8	8.1	6.7	7.0	6.0

[1] Preliminary.

Sources: Singapore, Department of Statistics: *Singapore National Accounts, 1960-1973* (Singapore, Singapore National Printers, 1975), p. 35; idem: *Yearbook of Statistics, 1980/81* (Singapore, Singapore National Printers, 1981), p. 66; idem: *Yearbook of Statistics, 1982/83* (Singapore, Singapore National Printers, 1983), p. 78.

Table 9. Rate of employment growth by industrial sector, 1957-82 (percentages)

Industrial sector	1957-66	1966-70	1970-80	1980-82
Total	1.7	4.4	5.2	3.3
Agriculture and fishing	-5.6	4.0	-2.8	-9.6
Quarrying	-1.4	11.5	-6.2	26.7
Manufacturing	3.5	8.2	8.5	3.7
Utilities	7.1	0.3	1.1	-9.7
Construction	5.1	5.7	5.3	11.2
Trade	-0.5	4.4	4.2	1.8
Transport and communications	1.0	10.0	4.3	3.0
Services	3.0	0.8	4.3	3.8
Activities not adequately defined	–	–	–	-27.2

Sources: Singapore, Department of Statistics: *Report on the Census of Population, 1957* (Singapore, Government Printer, 1964), p. 84; Singapore, Ministry of National Development and Economic Research Centre: *Singapore Sample Household Survey, 1966* (Singapore, Government Printing Office, 1967), pp. 132-137; Singapore, Department of Statistics: *Report on the Census of Population, 1970*, Vol. II (Singapore, Government Printing Office, 1973), p. 89; idem: *Census on the Population, 1980*, Release No. 4 (Singapore, Singapore National Printers, 1981), p. 13; Singapore, Ministry of Labour: *Report on the Labour Force Survey of Singapore, 1980* (Singapore, Photoplates Private Ltd., 1981), p. 59; idem: *Report on the Labour Force Survey of Singapore, 1982* (Singapore, Photoplates Private Ltd., 1983), p. 47.

The high rate of growth in construction in the 1960s reflects heavy public sector construction of housing and infrastructure such as expanded port facilities, industrial estates, roads, schools and so on. The growth spurt in manufacturing and financial and business services in the late 1960s and early 1970s reflects the take-off in export manufacturing, and in banking and finance, respectively. Multinational firms were prominent investors in both these sectors. In the 1970s transport and communications became the fastest growing sector, reflecting Singapore's development as the world's second busiest sea port and a major air services centre, and its increasing importance in international and regional communications networks.

Employment grew more slowly than output. Between 1957 and 1966 it grew by only 1.7 per cent a year, compared to an estimated annual GDP growth rate for the period of around 4 per cent (see table 9). Between 1966 and 1970 employment growth increased to 4.4 per cent a year, with quarrying, transport and communications and manufacturing experiencing the largest increases. Employment growth in manufacturing was nearly twice as fast as in the economy as a whole, and by the 1970s this was the fastest growing sector in terms of employment, reflecting its high labour-intensity. However, manufacturing employment growth at 8.5 per cent a year in the 1970s was still less than output growth at 10 per cent a year during the same decade.

Tables 10 and 11 present principal statistics of the manufacturing sector for the past 21 years. In 1981 there were more than six times as many manufacturing establishments as there were in 1960. The number of workers they employed increased more than tenfold between 1960 and 1981, an annual growth rate of 11.7 per cent, or about half the rate of growth in output and value-added (in current dollars). Average employee remuneration nearly quadrupled in

Table 10. Principal statistics of manufacturing, 1960-81

	1960	1965	1970 [1]	1975	1980 [2]	1981
Number of establishments	548	1 000	1 747	2 385	3 355	3 439
Number of workers	27 416	47 334	120 509	191 528	285 250	281 675
Materials (S$m)	302.8	693.3	2 668.4	8 586.0	21 415.2	24 891.5
Output (S$m)	465.6	1 086.4	3 891.0	12 610.1	31 657.9	36 787.1
Value-added (S$m)	142.1	348.4	1 093.7	3 411.1	8 521.9	9 720.5
Sales (S$m)						
Total	457.0	1 075.5	3 846.2	12 401.0	30 946.7	36 543.5
Direct exports	164.3	349.2	1 523.0	7 200.7	19 172.9	22 375.3
Employees' remuneration (S$m)	66.8	131.7	397.6	1 180.5	2 526.9	2 938.1
Capital expenditure (S$m)	9.8	59.2	421.3	622.6	1 861.9	1 966.8

[1] Prior to 1970 data included repair and servicing of motor vehicles and other household goods and carpentry and joinery work which accounted for about 0.6 per cent of output and 1.0 per cent of value-added in 1969.   [2] Prior to 1980, data on output and sales of petroleum refining industry included the value of products processed for third party overseas.
Source: Singapore, Department of Statistics: *Report on the Census of Industrial Production, 1981* (Singapore, Singapore National Printers, 1982), p. 1.

Table 11. Rate of growth of principal statistics of manufacturing, 1960-81 (percentages)

	1960-65	1966-70 [1]	1960-70 [1]	1971-75	1976-81 [2]	1971-81 [2]	1960-81 [1,2]
Number of establishments	12.8	11.7	12.3	7.1	6.5	6.6	9.1
Number of workers	11.5	22.9	16.0	8.0	6.3	7.2	11.7
Materials	18.0	32.3	24.3	28.5	18.6	23.0	23.4
Output	18.5	30.9	23.7	28.0	19.2	22.8	23.1
Value-added	19.7	27.4	22.6	25.7	19.7	21.7	22.3
Sales							
Total	18.7	30.8	23.7	27.8	18.6	22.9	23.2
Direct exports	16.3	39.3	24.9	38.6	18.5	27.6	26.4
Employees' remuneration	14.6	27.4	19.5	23.8	17.5	19.3	19.7
Capital expenditure	43.3	53.7	45.7	7.8	26.0	15.6	28.7

[1] Prior to 1970 data included repair and servicing of motor vehicles and other household goods and carpentry and joinery work which accounted for about 0.6 per cent of output and 1.0 per cent of value added in 1969.   [2] Prior to 1980, data on output and sales of petroleum refining industry included the value of products processed for third party overseas.
Source: Singapore, Department of Statistics: *Report on the Census of Industrial Production, 1981* (Singapore, Singapore National Printers, 1982), p. 1.

money terms during the period. Exports rose from 36 per cent of sales in 1960 to 61 per cent of sales in 1981.

Tables 12 and 13 show manufacturing output and its growth by three-digit industries. In 1960, with the exception of petroleum refining and products, which ranked second to food, the largest manufacturing industries produced simple consumer goods – food, beverages, cigarettes – for the domestic market. By 1970 petroleum accounted for 31 per cent of all manufacturing output, most of which was exported. Food was the second largest industry, accounting for 14

Table 12. Manufacturing output by three-digit industries, 1960-81 (S$'000)

Industrial Code	Industry major group	1960	1965	1970	1975	1980	1981
311-2	Food	75 318	155 000	551 361	843 528	1 661 501	1 692 519
313	Beverages	39 331	48 735	66 431	130 524	249 146	327 213
314	Cigarettes and other tobacco products	38 904	79 187	97 583	144 453	171 296	193 647
321	Textiles and textile manufactures			84 387	259 653	488 809	422 064
322	Wearing apparel except footwear	15 208	47 647	86 044	286 064	848 395	924 734
323	Leather and leather products			14 692	21 986	46 960	49 631
324	Footwear			17 943	30 336	53 603	54 929
331	Sawn timber and other wood products except furniture	35 697	65 808	186 464	311 294	749 775	640 997
332	Furniture and fixtures except primarily of metal	3 842	10 945	24 026	48 903	227 539	277 090
341	Paper and paper products	5 187	10 823	37 757	96 838	272 709	302 216
342	Printing and publishing	42 674	61 777	98 322	225 224	550 420	674 267
351	Industrial chemicals and gases			34 902	142 866	346 085	363 674
352	Paints, pharmaceutical and other chemical products	63 626	260 984	77 717	274 840	583 261	663 391
353-4	Petroleum refineries and petroleum products	18 138[1]	21 828[1]	1 221 821	4 753 331	11 520 518	14 453 833
355	Processing of jelutong and gum damar			14 610	20 151	25 863	28 226
356	Rubber products except rubber footwear			39 534	54 298	89 741	76 270
357	Plastic products		—	35 174	131 920	498 116	518 962
361-2	Pottery, china, earthenware and glass products			17 858	28 296	68 049	90 345
363	Bricks, tiles and other structural clay products			8 424	16 205	30 703	34 901
364	Cement and cement additives	17 310	51 091	35 992	158 046	277 097	347 188
365	Structural cement and concrete products			11 098	58 168	156 459	263 942
369	Asbestos, stone and other non-metallic mineral products			16 471	88 387	115 394	138 150
371	Iron and steel			50 501	145 193	338 131	343 102
372	Zinc and other non-ferrous metals	4 926	27 450	24 998	41 330	190 445	130 529
381	Metal grills, cans, pipes and other fabricated products	30 389	93 887	217 967	489 145	1 234 858	1 492 664
382	Calculators, refrigerators, air-conditioners and industrial machinery	16 805	19 953	74 568	651 492	1 662 677	2 484 207
383	Radios, televisions, semi-conductors and other electrical machinery	17 090	25 479	283 012	1 486 465	6 318 434	6 778 743

(table concluded overleaf)

Table 12: (concl.)

Industrial Code	Industry major group	1960	1965	1970	1975	1980	1981
384	Transport equipment and oil rigs	31 708	67 714	329 952	1 337 166	2 043 458	2 223 838
385	Professional and scientific equipment and photographic and optical goods	–	–	12 469	182 297	382 804	290 627
390	Other manufacturing industries (jewellery, toys, umbrellas, etc.)	9 416 [2]	38 058 [2]	118 933	151 746	455 648	505 197
	Total manufacturing excluding rubber processing	465 568	1 086 363	3 891 012	12 610 144	31 657 895	36 787 096

[1] Includes rubber footwear. [2] Includes plastic products.

Sources: Singapore, Department of Statistics: *Report on the Census of Industrial Production, 1960/61* (Singapore, Government Printing Office, 1964), p. 36; idem: *Report on the Census of Industrial Production, 1965* (Singapore, Government Printing Office, 1966), p. 19; idem: *Report on the Census of Industrial Production, 1981* (Singapore, Namic Printers Pte. Ltd., 1982), pp. 14-15.

Table 13. Rate of growth of manufacturing output by three-digit industries, 1960-81 (percentages)

Industrial code	Industry major group	1960-65	1966-70	1960-70	1971-75	1976-81	1971-81	1960-81
311-2	Food	15.5	32.2	22.0	9.9	12.5	11.3	16.0
313	Beverages	4.4	4.1	5.4	16.8	16.8	16.7	10.6
314	Cigarettes and other tobacco products	15.3	4.3	9.6	11.4	4.7	7.5	7.9
321	Textiles and textile manufactures				19.2	3.2	12.6	
322	Wearing apparel except footwear	25.7	35.8	29.6	23.6	17.9	22.4	24.2
323	Leather and leather products				12.6	9.8	13.7	
324	Footwear				6.4	10.1	8.8	
331	Sawn timber and other wood products except furniture	13.0	22.0	18.0	11.8	8.7	12.4	14.7
332	Furniture and fixtures except primarily of metal	23.3	14.7	20.1	13.4	35.2	25.1	22.6
341	Paper and paper products	15.9	10.6	22.0	21.5	21.4	21.1	21.4
342	Printing and publishing	7.7	10.7	8.7	17.7	18.4	19.1	14.0
351	Industrial chemicals and gases				33.1	11.6	21.8	
352	Paints, pharmaceutical and other chemical products	32.6	39.1	35.6	32.9	16.3	22.4	29.9

Code	Industry							
353–4	Petroleum refineries and petroleum products	3.8[1]			32.2	18.8	25.0	
355	Processing of jelutong and gum damar	18.0[1]		11.6	11.8	11.5	8.1	8.7
356	Rubber products except rubber footwear	—			5.3	5.7	5.6	
357	Plastic products	—		—	27.7	26.4	27.9	—
361–2	Pottery, china, earthenware and glass products				18.8	19.5	20.3	
363	Bricks, tiles and other structural clay products				9.7	11.6	12.0	
364	Cement and cement additives	24.2		17.9	39.7	16.5	23.8	20.5
365	Structural cement and concrete products	10.1			46.0	32.6	35.3	
369	Asbestos, stone and other non-metallic mineral products				27.4	10.2	15.2	
371	Iron and steel	41.0		31.4	26.3	17.6	19.7	24.3
372	Zinc and other non-ferrous metals	13.7			17.0	31.0	19.5	
381	Metal grills, cans, pipes and other fabricated products	25.3	23.5	21.8	21.8	24.1	21.0	20.4
382	Calculators, refrigerators, air-conditioners and industrial machinery	3.5	30.6	16.1	65.0	29.7	33.5	26.9
383	Radios, televisions, semi-conductors and other electrical machinery	8.3	70.6	32.4	38.8	32.0	32.8	33.0
384	Transport equipment and oil rigs	16.4	42.8	26.4	32.8	14.8	19.2	22.4
385	Professional and scientific equipment and photographic and optical goods			—	63.4	8.5	27.5	—
390	Other manufacturing industries (jewellery, toys, umbrellas, etc.)	32.2[2]	27.4[2]	28.9	4.9	23.4	14.9	20.9
	Total manufacturing excluding rubber processing	18.5	30.9	23.7	28.0	19.2	22.8	23.1

Sources and notes: Same as table 12.

per cent. Next in importance were various other export-oriented industries: electrical and electronic products, transport equipment and oil rigs (shipbuilding), textiles and garments. In 1981 except for food the rankings remained the same, with petroleum increasing its share of 43 per cent (reflecting the increase in oil prices in the 1970s). The electrical and electronics industry accounted for 22 per cent (39 per cent if petroleum – a primary processing industry – were excluded), followed by shipbuilding, food and textiles and garments. Over the period 1960-81 the electronics industry grew most rapidly, followed by petroleum, and by the other export-oriented industries (table 13).

Table 14 shows manufacturing employment by three-digit industries. In 1960 printing and publishing employed the most people, followed by food, and the timber industry. By 1970 the transport equipment industry (which includes oil rig construction) was the largest employer, followed by the electrical and electronics industry, and then by textiles and garments. In 1981 the electrical and electronics industry was by far the largest employer, followed by textiles and garments, and then by transport equipment and oil rigs. Together, these labour-intensive export industries employed nearly two-thirds of all workers in the manufacturing sector. Table 15 shows that they experienced the most rapid increase in employment between 1960 and 1981.

For textiles and garments the increase in employment was greatest between 1960 and 1965, declining to below-average growth in the 1970s. In the latter half of the 1970s employment in the textile sector actually declined absolutely. The other export industries experienced their greatest employment growth between 1966 and 1970. The electrical and electronics industries maintained above-average employment growth rates throughout the 1970s, but employment growth in transport equipment and oil rigs was very slow in the late 1970s. Overall, manufacturing employment grew by 11.7 per cent a year between 1960 and 1981.

Direct exports in manufacturing increased tenfold between 1970 and 1981 (table 16), raising the proportion of total sales exported from 39.6 per cent in 1970 to 61.2 per cent in 1981. Next to petroleum, electronics, transport equipment and oil rigs, food, electrical products and wearing apparel contributed the most to exports. All these industries except textiles increased their export orientation over the period, from 47.7 per cent of sales to 66.9 per cent for petroleum, from 77.3 per cent to 83.1 per cent for electronics, from 31.3 per cent to 46.6 per cent for transport equipment and oil rigs, and 64.7 per cent to 71.2 per cent for wearing apparel. Throughout the period electronics was the most heavily export-oriented industry. Total manufacturing exports increased at the average rate of 28.8 per cent a year in the 1970s.

Manufactures account for almost all of Singapore's domestic exports, as shown in table 17. Electrical and electronic products, and output of the shipbuilding industry, are mostly included in the category "machinery and transport", which is second only to "mineral fuels", or petroleum. Together these two commodity groups accounted for some 71 per cent of all domestic exports in 1982. The structure of retained imports (table 18) also reflects the importance of export manufacturing. In 1982 the largest component of retained imports was "mineral

Table 14. Manufacturing employment by three-digit industries, 1960–81 (numbers)

Industrial code	Industry major group	1960	1965	1970	1975	1980	1981
311-2	Food	3 664	5 049	9 062	8 725	10 053	10 075
313	Beverages	1 667	1 944	2 348	2 640	2 650	2 744
314	Cigarettes and other tobacco products	965	1 247	1 048	1 301	1 277	976
321	Textiles and textile manufactures			7 051	11 380	9 710	7 906
322	Wearing apparel except footwear	1 302	6 138	9 987	17 966	27 188	27 870
323	Leather and leather products			713	863	1 244	1 186
324	Footwear			2 005	1 901	1 524	1 428
331	Sawn timber and other wood products except furniture	2 512	4 647	9 200	9 420	10 376	8 291
332	Furniture and fixtures except primarily of metal	431	970	1 795	2 640	6 145	6 561
341	Paper and paper products	439	873	2 563	3 366	4 294	4 495
342	Printing and publishing	4 061	4 637	7 015	8 511	12 101	12 487
351	Industrial chemicals and gases			814	1 450	2 138	2 058
352	Paints, pharmaceutical and other chemical products	1 437	2 249	3 059	3 574	4 300	4 291
353-4	Petroleum refineries and petroleum products			2 199	3 331	3 342	3 511
355	Processing of jelutong and gum damar	877 [1]	1 355 [1]	243	205	145	157
356	Rubber products except rubber footwear			1 635	1 462	1 941	1 359
357	Plastic products	–	–	2 186	4 969	9 225	9 121
361-2	Pottery, china, earthenware and glass products			1 795	684	955	1 133
363	Bricks, tiles and other structural clay products			1 179	815	474	461
364	Cement and cement additives	2 374	3 169	428	581	461	474
365	Structural cement and concrete products			597	1 185	1 458	1 730
369	Asbestos, stone and other non-metallic mineral products			839	1 700	1 315	1 261
371	Iron and steel	471	1 076	1 078	1 410	1 878	1 920
372	Zinc and other non-ferrous metals			414	445	459	449
381	Metal grills, cans, pipes and other fabricated products	1 724	4 276	8 691	10 975	17 669	19 481
382	Calculators, refrigerators, air-conditioners and industrial machinery	1 448	1 393	3 809	13 682	20 274	23 963
383	Radios, televisions, semi-conductors and other electrical machinery	1 252	1 454	13 586	34 556	87 660	85 499

(table concluded overleaf)

Table 14: (concl.)

Industrial code	Industry major group	1960	1965	1970	1975	1980	1981
384	Transport equipment and oil rigs	2 270	4 952	16 213	30 421	27 420	28 491
385	Professional and scientific equipment and photographic and optical goods	–	–	886	6 941	10 456	5 419
390	Other manufacturing industries (jewellery, toys, umbrellas, etc.)	522 [2]	1 905 [2]	8 071	4 429	7 118	6 878
	Total manufacturing excluding rubber processing	27 416	47 334	120 509	191 528	285 250	281 675

[1] Includes rubber footwear.   [2] Includes plastic products.

Sources: Singapore, Department of Statistics: *Report on the Census of Industrial Production 1960/61* (Singapore, Government Printing Office, 1964), p. 36; idem: *Report on the Census of Industrial Production 1965* (Singapore, Government Printing Office, 1966), p. 19; idem: *Report on the Census of Industrial Production 1981* (Singapore, Namic Printers Pte Ltd., 1982), pp. 12-13.

Table 15.   Rate of growth of manufacturing employment by three-digit industries, 1960-81 (percentages)

Industrial code	Industry major group	1960-65	1966-70	1960-70	1971-75	1976-81	1971-81	1960-81
311-2	Food	6.6	13.8	9.5	-2.6	3.3	0.4	4.9
313	Beverages	3.1	4.2	3.5	2.9	0.8	1.5	2.4
314	Cigarettes and other tobacco products	5.3	-3.9	0.8	6.4	-3.7	-0.4	0.1
321	Textiles and textile manufactures				6.5	-7.4	-1.1	
322	Wearing apparel except footwear	36.4	28.6	31.3	7.6	6.2	7.6	17.5
323	Leather and leather products				3.7	4.2	4.7	
324	Footwear				-3.5	-3.9	-4.2	
331	Sawn timber and other wood products except furniture	13.1	27.3	13.9	-3.4	-1.1	-2.6	5.9
332	Furniture and fixtures except primarily of metal	17.6	13.1	15.4	6.3	17.5	12.2	13.8
341	Paper and paper products	14.7	24.0	19.3	5.7	4.4	5.2	11.7

Code	Industry							
342	Printing and publishing	2.7	10.0	5.6	3.8	6.6	5.5	5.5
351	Industrial chemicals and gases	9.4	27.2	15.5	8.8	5.8	6.5	9.6
352	Paints, pharmaceutical and other chemical products				4.2	4.3	3.6	
353-4	Petroleum refineries and petroleum products				7.2	2.1	3.3	
355	Processing of jelutong and gum damar	9.1[1]	5.6[1]	7.9	-2.0	-0.9	-3.4	2.6
356	Rubber products except rubber footwear				-3.7	-1.7	-2.2	
357	Plastic products			–	13.6	11.3	12.1	–
361-2	Pottery, china, earthenware and glass products				-8.5	7.5	1.5	
363	Bricks, tiles and other structural clay products				-5.1	-12.5	-7.5	
364	Cement and cement additives	6.0	7.4	7.4	7.4	-3.9	1.1	3.7
365	Structural cement and concrete products				20.8	9.0	12.0	
369	Asbestos, stone and other non-metallic mineral products				9.0	-6.2	0.5	
371	Iron and steel	18.0	-1.0	12.2	3.0	4.8	4.4	8.0
372	Zinc and other non-ferrous metals				-5.1	26.4	-2.0	
381	Metal grills, cans, pipes and other fabricated products	19.9	21.8	17.6	4.8	10.4	7.9	12.2
382	Calculators, refrigerators, air-conditioners and industrial machinery	-0.8	20.8	10.2	32.4	8.5	13.7	14.3
383	Radios, televisions, semi-conductors and other electrical machinery	3.0	70.4	27.0	16.5	11.6	20.6	22.3
384	Transport equipment and oil rigs	16.9	32.8	21.7	10.5	3.2	4.4	12.8
385	Professional and scientific equipment and photographic and optical goods				52.4	-6.0	15.5	–
390	Other manufacturing industries (jewellery, toys, umbrellas, etc.)	29.5[2]	40.4[2]	31.5	-13.4	8.6	-1.4	13.1
	Total manufacturing excluding rubber processing	11.5	22.9	16.0	8.0	6.3	7.2	11.7

Sources and notes : Same as table 8.

Table 16.   Direct exports by three-digit industries, 1970-81 (S$'000) (value and ratio/percentage of total sales)

Industrial code	Industry major group	1970		1975		1980		1981	
		Value	Ratio	Value	Ratio	Value	Ratio	Value	Ratio
311-2	Food	185 674	33.2	317 558	37.2	871 662	52.0	877 599	50.3
313	Beverages	13 127	19.8	31 305	23.7	55 758	22.6	96 209	29.2
314	Cigarettes and other tobacco products	4 040	4.2	2 506	1.7	17 947	10.4	22 099	11.6
321	Textiles and textile manufactures	40 831	50.0	141 541	55.0	238 045	50.1	199 679	47.5
322	Wearing apparel except footwear	55 459	64.7	197 830	69.4	602 335	71.0	652 995	71.2
323	Leather and leather products	8 303	54.4	12 128	52.9	19 604	40.7	21 871	41.1
324	Footwear	4 078	22.3	12 573	38.7	20 037	38.1	19 124	34.6
331	Sawn timber and other wood products except furniture	84 848	46.3	195 779	61.3	408 378	54.6	324 298	51.1
332	Furniture and fixtures except primarily of metal	2 456	10.2	12 959	25.9	97 157	44.2	137 636	50.7
341	Paper and paper products	5 893	15.5	11 149	11.2	24 215	9.1	35 516	11.8
342	Printing and publishing	13 189	13.8	45 550	19.7	99 225	18.1	113 760	17.1
351	Industrial chemicals and gases	5 167	15.0	34 621	23.9	179 086	52.2	163 421	45.8
352	Paints, pharmaceutical and other chemical products	22 147	28.4	148 410	55.7	353 023	61.9	383 855	58.1
353-4	Petroleum refineries and petroleum products	580 073	47.7	3 102 654	66.2	7 618 813	67.3	9 612 989	66.9
355	Processing of jelutong and gum damar	10 756	72.9	14 665	70.9	16 017	63.4	18 009	61.9
356	Rubber products except rubber footwear	14 879	36.7	18 420	32.0	46 362	48.2	31 779	42.1
357	Plastic products	10 206	30.1	35 022	26.3	107 152	21.9	117 310	22.8
361-2	Pottery, china, earthenware and glass products	8 437	48.4	11 436	40.9	36 726	55.7	46 382	56.2
363	Bricks, tiles and other structural clay products	119	1.6	200	1.2	649	2.1	881	2.5
364	Cement and cement additives	1 496	4.1	27 196	16.9	74 836	26.6	85 315	24.2
365	Structural cement and concrete products	–	–	–	–	1 491	0.8	799	0.3
369	Asbestos, stone and other non-metallic mineral products	15 220	64.4	40 529	46.7	24 317	21.4	29 983	21.7
371	Iron and steel	1 792	3.6	15 009	10.8	72 530	22.0	53 310	14.7
372	Zinc and other non-ferrous metals	14 130	57.5	18 964	43.5	144 246	76.7	81 191	63.8
381	Metal grills, cans, pipes and other fabricated products	50 979	24.2	149 309	30.3	354 880	29.4	409 833	27.4

382	Calculators, refrigerators, air-conditioners and industrial machinery	16 957	24.6	477 049	73.8	1 085 992	68.9	1 684 131	72.7
383	Radios, televisions, semi-conductors and other electrical machinery	212 049	77.3	1 255 096	85.5	5 093 044	83.1	5 687 687	83.1
384	Transport equipment and oil rigs	98 533	31.3	671 410	56.9	968 814	51.2	996 537	46.6
385	Professional and scientific equipment and photographic and optical goods	5 900	48.0	153 100	78.9	336 793	91.7	257 745	90.2
390	Other manufacturing industries (jewellery, toys, umbrellas, etc.)	36 296	31.9	46 725	31.1	203 780	46.3	213 307	42.9
	Total manufacturing excluding rubber processing	1 523 033	39.6	7 200 693	58.1	19 172 916	62.0	22 375 250	61.2

Sources: Singapore, Department of Statistics: *Report on the Census of Industrial Production 1970* (Singapore, Government Printing Office, 1972), pp. 10-11; idem: *Report on the Census of Industrial Production 1975* (Singapore, Photoplates Pte Ltd., 1976), pp. 12-13; idem: *Report on the Census of Industrial Production 1980* (Singapore, Singapore National Printers, 1981), pp. 30-31; idem: *Report on the Census of Industrial Production 1981* (Singapore, Namic Printers Pte Ltd., 1982), pp. 30-31.

Table 17.   Domestic exports by commodity, 1970-82 (S$m)

Commodity	1970	1975	1980	1982
Total	1 832.2	7 540.4	25 805.2	29 157.8
Food	105.4	278.1	600.6	449.5
Beverages and tobacco	11.8	25.8	102.7	134.1
Crude materials [1]	29.9	44.9	152.3	125.3
Mineral fuels [2]	792.2	3 233.1	11 612.2	13 846.5
Animal and vegetable oils	48.8	56.1	393.7	482.6
Chemicals	43.3	208.2	572.9	690.7
Manufactured goods by materials	169.9	486.2	1 322.7	1 214.4
Machinery and transport	197.6	1 686.5	6 566.6	6 961.0
Miscellaneous manufactured articles	144.5	668.3	1 886.5	1 907.2
Miscellaneous transactions n.e.s.	288.8	853.2	2 595.1	3 346.5

[1] Excludes processed rubber and sawn timber.   [2] Figures from 1975 include petroleum naphtha which was previously included under chemicals.
Sources: Singapore, Department of Statistics: *Yearbook of Statistics 1980/81* (Singapore, Singapore National Printers, 1981), p. 134; idem: *Yearbook of Statistics 1982/83* (Singapore, Singapore National Printers, 1983), p. 146.

Table 18.   Retained imports by commodity, 1960-82 (S$m)

Commodity	1960	1970	1980	1982 [1]
Total	817.7	4 610.2	35 697.7	44 929.6
Food	263.1	506.3	1 507.9	1 663.4
Beverages and tobacco	21.6	68.1	221.4	256.6
Crude materials	−28.5	−541.5	−1 130.8	−349.7
Mineral fuels	199.2	984.5	14 535.7	19 709.5
Animal and vegetable oils	9.2	34.6	299.2	373.8
Chemicals	67.2	301.3	1 841.1	1 759.0
Manufactured goods	205.2	1 397.7	5 118.2	5 783.1
Machinery and equipment	69.6	1 395.1	10 781.0	12 634.1
Miscellaneous manufactures	139.8	435.3	2 265.2	2 928.0
Miscellaneous	−128.7	28.8	258.8	171.8

[1] Preliminary.
Source: Singapore, Ministry of Trade and Industry: *Economic Survey of Singapore, 1982* (Singapore, Singapore National Printers, 1983), pp. 110-112.

fuels", input for the export-oriented petroleum refining industry, followed by "machinery and equipment", much of which consists of equipment and inputs for other export manufacturing industries. Although Singapore is heavily dependent on imports to supply the domestic market with most consumption as well as investment goods, "manufactured goods" and "miscellaneous manufactures" rank only third and fourth among retained imports in 1982. This contrasts with the position in 1960 when, next to food, "manufactured goods" were the largest component of retained imports.

Tables 19 and 20 show the destination of domestic exports, and reflect their commodity composition. Besides the neighbouring parts of South-East Asia, most of Singapore's domestic exports go to the developed countries of Europe, North America and Japan, which are both the parent countries of the multinationals which manufacture for export from Singapore, and the primary markets for these manufactures. In 1970 Malaysia was still Singapore's largest export market, the natural extension of the domestic market for import-substituting manufacturing industries and other industries. By 1975 it had been overtaken by the United States, Japan and Hong Kong. In 1982 Malaysia ranked third after Japan and the United States. While much of the exports to Japan consist of refined petroleum from the Middle East, most of the exports to the United States

Table 19.   Domestic exports by region, 1970-82 (S$m)

Region	1970	1975	1980	1982
Total	1 832.2	7 540.4	25 805.2	29 157.8
South-East Asia	698.5	1 325.1	4 382.9	5 637.9
North-East Asia	348.5	1 760.6	6 476.6	7 902.4
South Asia	36.6	164.2	1 411.7	1 672.4
West Asia	36.7	368.9	1 449.4	1 611.2
EEC	215.3	1 087.8	3 078.0	2 997.5
EFTA	28.7	141.6	357.5	302.5
Other Western Europe	31.9	77.5	280.9	65.5
Socialist countries of Eastern Europe	30.0	69.2	171.6	201.9
North America	215.6	1 244.0	4 028.4	4 330.7
LAFTA	0.2	21.8	468.5	84.5
Oceania	120.9	891.6	2 815.3	2 681.3
Rest of the world	69.7	388.2	884.4	1 670.0

Sources: Singapore, Department of Statistics: *Yearbook of Statistics, 1980/81* (Singapore, Singapore National Printers, 1981), pp. 130-131; idem: *Yearbook of Statistics, 1982/83* (Singapore, Singapore National Printers, 1983), pp. 142-143.

Table 20.   Domestic exports by selected country, 1970-82 (S$m)

Country or area	1970		1975		1980		1982	
	Value	% of total domestic exports	Value	% of total domestic exports	Value	% of total domestic exports	Value	% of total domestic exports
United States	204.2	11.1	1 177.2	15.6	3 894.1	15.1	4 196.2	14.4
Japan	216.5	11.8	917.2	12.2	2 877.4	11.2	4 253.1	14.6
Hong Kong	122.6	6.7	752.5	10.0	2 659.4	10.3	2 751.0	9.4
Malaysia	217.8	11.9	672.5	8.9	2 254.3	8.7	3 618.4	12.4
Australia	69.5	3.8	422.4	5.6	1 344.8	5.2	1 299.4	4.5
United Kingdom	113.9	6.2	334.3	4.4	690.1	2.7	648.1	2.2

Sources: Singapore, Department of Statistics: *Yearbook of Statistics, 1980/81* (Singapore, Singapore National Printers, 1981), pp. 130-131; idem: *Yearbook of Statistics, 1982/83* (Singapore, Singapore National Printers, 1983), pp. 142-143.

Table 21.   Retained imports by region, 1970-82 (S$m)

Region	1970	1975	1980	1982
Total	4 610.2	14 052.9	35 697.7	44 929.6
South-East Asia	692.5	774.3	3 727.1	4 325.4
North-East Asia	1 848.7	4 279.9	11 261.5	13 496.9
South Asia	88.8	68.0	−537.7	−74.2
West Asia	630.4	3 943.6	10 704.9	13 093.7
EEC	646.9	1 879.6	3 782.8	5 049.4
EFTA	126.9	331.4	1 052.2	1 086.9
Other Western Europe	−67.6	−50.3	−168.9	23.4
Socialist countries of Eastern Europe	−133.6	−93.0	−390.6	−111.9
North America	220.3	2 473.2	5 983.5	6 448.1
LAFTA	−31.4	−48.5	215.1	180.7
Oceania	280.6	478.1	946.6	1 054.7
Rest of the world	41.1	16.7	−878.6	356.5

Sources: Singapore, Department of Statistics: *Yearbook of Statistics, 1980/81* (Singapore, Singapore National Printers, 1981), pp. 126-131; idem: *Yearbook of Statistics, 1982/83* (Singapore, Singapore National Printers, 1983), pp. 138-143.

Table 22.   Retained imports by selected country, 1970-82 (S$m)

Country	1970	1975	1980	1982
Japan	1 313.0	3 058.6	8 755.5	10 200.2
Saudi Arabia	70.8	1 626.8	6 055.4	8 642.8
United States	491.7	2 425.8	5 859.3	6 378.3
Malaysia	581.6	722.8	3 151.9	3 825.1
Kuwait	357.5	587.9	2 751.3	850.6
Iran	161.6	958.4	333.5	1 886.3
United Kingdom	358.5	750.5	1 392.1	1 451.8

Sources: Singapore, Department of Statistics: *Yearbook of Statistics, 1980/81* (Singapore, Singapore National Printers, 1981), pp. 126-131; idem: *Yearbook of Statistics, 1982/83* (Singapore, Singapore National Printers, 1983), pp. 138-143.

consist of other manufactured products, most notably electrical and electronic goods.

The regional and country origin of retained imports (tables 21 and 22) also reflects the needs of the export manufacturing industries. Imports of crude petroleum from Saudi Arabia and Kuwait loom large in the retained import bill. Purchases from Japan and the United States include, besides consumer goods for domestic consumption, machinery, equipment and material inputs for the manufacturing sector.

With the growth of manufacturing industries which are both heavily import-dependent and export-oriented, trade patterns which once mainly reflected Singapore's entrepot role have changed. Retained imports have risen as a proportion of total imports (61 per cent in 1970 to 75 per cent in 1982), and

Table 23. Volume index of imports and exports, 1973-80 (1972 = 100)

Commodity	1973		1974		1975		1976		1977		1978		1979		1980	
	Imports	Exports	Imports	Exports	Imports	Exports	Imports	Exports	Imports	Exports	Imports	Exports	Imports	Exports	Imports	Exports
Total	114	122	130	134	122	123	133	146	143	169	159	189	185	227	213	266
Food	100	93	97	96	101	102	105	96	112	121	114	135	128	149	128	155
Beverages and tobacco	88	58	90	59	88	59	88	66	88	85	97	121	103	145	124	153
Crude materials	122	120	120	117	101	101	134	116	131	123	130	125	142	129	136	124
Mineral fuels	104	105	97	111	82	86	96	91	98	111	105	123	111	138	107	136
Animal and vegetable oils	107	102	118	98	64	69	76	82	79	104	53	88	117	165	76	215
Chemicals	122	128	135	128	119	88	130	118	147	140	181	175	210	200	217	200
Manufactured goods	114	124	124	119	121	133	119	159	126	169	149	224	163	240	183	276
Machinery and equipment	123	154	170	204	155	178	174	202	188	256	220	322	243	404	315	527
Miscellaneous manufactures	117	130	124	111	143	91	166	124	150	131	133	161	154	168	167	160
Miscellaneous	118	114	152	150	136	122	132	161	157	216	160	261	167	262	219	312

Sources: Singapore, Department of Statistics: *Yearbook of Statistics, 1979/80* (Singapore, Singapore National Printers, 1980), p. 139; idem: *Yearbook of Statistics, 1980/81* (Singapore, Singapore National Printers, 1981), p. 141.

Table 24. *Unit value index of imports and exports, 1973-80 (1972 = 100)*

Commodity	1973		1974		1975		1976		1977		1978		1979		1980	
	Imports	Exports	Imports	Exports	Imports	Exports	Imports	Exports	Imports	Exports	Imports	Exports	Imports	Exports	Imports	Exports
Total	116	123	167	175	167	170	175	181	189	196	195	203	210	217	246	249
Food	122	119	154	151	158	158	169	176	190	208	184	197	187	190	214	215
Beverages and tobacco	106	107	113	114	118	113	124	115	134	121	141	127	160	138	175	156
Crude materials	148	162	173	193	147	150	187	202	212	219	230	237	265	295	295	324
Mineral fuels	113	112	368	287	417	337	460	353	482	371	484	365	634	452	1 013	747
Animal and vegetable oils	116	111	226	240	216	231	178	196	247	296	257	390	255	350	239	345
Chemicals	122	133	190	209	191	198	177	257	183	271	180	255	203	270	243	332
Manufactured goods	116	125	152	152	150	138	145	143	150	159	160	171	178	192	199	203
Machinery and equipment	107	105	124	118	120	126	124	134	135	134	148	143	156	148	162	150
Miscellaneous manufactures	108	111	149	126	144	139	147	160	189	176	245	187	199	215	247	252
Miscellaneous	111	127	121	178	134	170	161	174	166	163	198	154	225	186	251	208

Sources: Singapore, Department of Statistics: *Yearbook of Statistics, 1979/80* (Singapore, Singapore National Printers, 1980), p. 140; idem: *Yearbook of Statistics, 1980/81* (Singapore, Singapore National Printers, 1981), p. 142.

domestic exports as a proportion of total exports (39 per cent in 1970 to 66 per cent in 1982). The change would be even more drastic if figures for 1960 were available.

Tables 23 and 24 present volume and value indices of imports and exports since 1973 (1972 = 100). They show that exports have risen about 25 per cent more than imports by volume, and about the same proportion by value. Since the figures are not broken down by domestic exports and retained imports only, the trend in the terms of trade for the domestic economy is not clear. However, the figures suggest that imports and exports of machinery and equipment have increased the most by volume, reflecting both Singapore's growth as an export manufacturing economy, and the industrialisation of its developing as well as developed country trading partners in the entrepot trade sector. The value indices show the sharp rise in the price of petroleum imports and exports, and a fairly small increase in the value of imports and exports of manufactured goods and machinery and equipment.

Table 25. Balance of payments, 1965-82 (S$m)

Major item	1965	1970	1975	1980	1982 [1]
A. Goods and services (net)	−101.2	−1 727.2	−1 536.0	−3 240.0	−2 553.1
Exports of goods and services	2 810.1	6 132.3	19 244.7	53 617.4	64 322.9
Imports of goods and services	3 569.9	7 859.5	20 780.7	56 857.4	66 876.0
Trade balance	−759.8	−2 619.4	−5 759.8	−9 055.8	−14 921.6
Balance of services	658.6	892.2	4 223.8	5 815.8	12 368.5
B. Transfer payments (net)	−48.9	−23.6	−92.3	−109.3	−184.1
Private	–	−63.5	−91.4	−97.6	−155.6
Government	–	39.9	−0.9	−11.7	−28.5
Current account balance	−150.1	−1 750.8	−1 628.3	−3 349.3	−2 737.2
C. Capital (net)	104.3	532.6	1 374.4	3 611.5	4 771.6
Non-monetary sector (net)	87.1	429.1	1 586.2	3 319.9	4 055.7
Private	57.8	349.9	1 565.3	3 352.6	4 087.6
Official	29.3	79.2	20.9	−32.7	−31.9
Monetary sector (net)	17.2	103.5	−211.8	291.6	715.9
Commercial banks:					
Foreign assets [2]	−154.6	−13.8	−464.1	−778.4	833.8
Foreign liabilities	171.8	117.3	252.3	1 070.0	−117.9
D. Allocation of special drawing rights	–	–	–	14.5	–
E. Balancing item	31.6	1 783.0	1 220.3	1 157.1	483.1
F. Overall balance (A+B+C+D+E)	−14.2	564.8	966.4	1 433.8	2 517.5
G. Official reserves (net) [2]	14.2	−564.8	−966.4	−1 433.8	−2 517.5
Special drawing rights	–	–	–	−8.3	−51.9
Reserve position in the Fund	–	–	–	−64.3	−10.1
Foreign exports assets	–	−564.8	−966.4	−1 361.2	−2 455.5

[1] Preliminary. [2] Increase in assets is indicated by a minus (−) sign.
Sources: Singapore, Department of Statistics: *Yearbook of Statistics, 1975/76* (Singapore, Singapore National Printers, 1977), p. 52; idem: *Yearbook of Statistics, 1982/83* (Singapore, Singapore National Printers, 1983), p. 85.

Singapore's role as an entrepot and services sector overwhelms its domestic trade in the balance of payments accounts (table 25). There is a persistent and growing deficit on the trade and current account balances. This deficit is covered by surpluses in the balance of services and in the capital account, giving an overall balance of payments surplus. Domestic manufactured exports are fairly unimportant for balance of payments reasons, given their high import intensity compared with the greater net importance of service and capital flows. Much of the capital inflows, however, are inflows into the export manufacturing sector.

Sectoral appraisal

The previous section has shown that manufacturing is a dynamic sector that has contributed greatly to Singapore's economic growth and employment expansion. Within manufacturing, the most dynamic subsectors are the export-oriented petroleum, electrical and electronics, and transport equipment industries. Whereas petroleum is the most important in terms of output value, electronics is the most important in terms of employment. All manufacturing industries rely heavily on foreign inputs, which are imported free of duty. Hence the net balance of payments contribution of the manufacturing sector as a whole, and even of its most export-oriented industries, is probably as large as the export statistics suggest. Growth of output and employment in all the export-oriented industries has varied with the world business cycle.

In all sectors and industries there has been a trend towards producing more skill- and capital-intensive products, with higher domestic value-added, mainly from skilled labour inputs and higher wages. Output per worker in manufacturing is highest in the petroleum industry, where it grew by 20 per cent a year between 1960 and 1970 (tables 26 and 27). Output per worker in the labour-intensive export manufacturing industries – textiles and garments, electrical and electronics, and transport equipment and oil rigs – is low, but has been growing at a respectable rate (13.9 per cent a year between 1971 and 1981 for textiles, 13.7 per cent for garments, 14.0 per cent for electrical and electronics, 14.1 per cent for transport equipment and oil rigs).

Though they rank low in terms of output per worker, the export-oriented, labour-intensive industries rank high in terms of value-added to output ratios (table 28). The value-added to output ratio for wearing apparel in 1981, for example, is 33.3 per cent compared with 11.8 per cent for petroleum. This reflects the fact that the wages of domestic labour are the major component of local value-added in wearing apparel and its low price (output value) on the world market.

As shown in table 29, capital expenditure per worker has been increasing throughout the manufacturing sector since 1960. Capital expenditure per worker is highest in the capital-intensive petroleum industry and relatively low in the labour-intensive electronics, transport equipment and textiles and garments industries. However, these industries – with the exception of garments – have a much higher ratio of capital spending to output than petroleum and than the average for the manufacturing sector as a whole (table 30).

Table 26. **Output per worker by three-digit industries, 1960-81 (S$'000)**

Industrial code	Industry major group	1960	1965	1970	1975	1980	1981
311-2	Food	20.6	30.7	60.8	96.7	165.3	168.0
313	Beverages	23.6	25.1	28.3	49.4	94.0	119.2
314	Cigarettes and other tobacco products	40.3	63.5	93.1	111.1	134.1	198.4
321	Textiles and textile manufactures			12.0	22.8	50.3	53.4
322	Wearing apparel except footwear	11.7	7.8	8.6	15.9	31.2	33.2
323	Leather and leather products			20.6	25.5	37.7	41.8
324	Footwear			8.9	15.9	35.2	38.5
331	Sawn timber and other wood products except furniture	14.2	14.2	20.3	33.0	72.3	77.3
332	Furniture and fixtures except primarily of metal	8.9	11.3	13.4	18.5	37.0	42.2
341	Paper and paper products	11.8	12.4	14.7	28.8	63.5	67.2
342	Printing and publishing	10.5	13.3	14.0	26.5	45.5	54.0
351	Industrial chemicals and gases			42.9	98.6	161.9	176.7
352	Paints, pharmaceutical and other chemical products	44.3	116.0	25.4	76.9	135.6	154.6
353-4	Petroleum refineries and petroleum products			555.6	1 427.0	3 447.2	4 116.7
355	Processing of jelutong and gum damar	20.7 [1]	16.1 [1]	60.1	98.5	178.4	179.8
356	Rubber products except rubber footwear			24.2	37.1	46.2	56.1
357	Plastic products	–	–	16.1	26.5	54.0	56.9
361-2	Pottery, china, earthenware and glass products			10.0	41.4	71.3	79.7
363	Bricks, tiles and other structural clay products			7.1	19.9	64.8	75.7
364	Cement and cement additives	7.3	16.1	84.1	271.9	601.1	732.5
365	Structural cement and concrete products			18.6	49.1	107.3	152.6
369	Asbestos, stone and other non-metallic mineral products			19.6	52.0	87.8	109.6
371	Iron and steel	10.5	25.5	46.8	103.0	180.0	178.7
372	Zinc and other non-ferrous metals			60.4	92.9	414.9	290.7
381	Metal grills, cans, pipes and other fabricated products	17.6	22.0	25.1	44.6	69.9	76.6
382	Calculators, refrigerators, air-conditioners and industrial machinery	11.6	14.3	19.6	47.6	82.0	103.7
383	Radios, televisions, semi-conductors and other electrical machinery	13.7	17.5	20.8	43.0	73.2	79.3
384	Transport equipment and oil rigs	14.0	13.7	20.4	44.0	74.5	78.1
385	Professional and scientific equipment and photographic and optical goods	–	–	14.1	26.3	36.6	53.6
390	Other manufacturing industries (jewellery, toys, umbrellas, etc.)	18.0 [2]	20.0 [2]	14.7	34.3	64.0	73.5
	Total manufacturing excluding rubber processing	17.0	23.0	32.3	65.8	111.0	130.6

[1] Includes rubber footwear.   [2] Includes plastic products.

Sources: Singapore, Department of Statistics: *Report on the Census of Industrial Production, 1960/61* (Singapore, Government Printing Office, 1964), p. 36; idem: *Report on the Census of Industrial Production, 1965* (Singapore, Government Printing Office, 1966), p. 19; idem: *Report on the Census of Industrial Production, 1981* (Singapore, Namic Printers Pte Ltd., 1982), pp. 24-25.

Table 27. *Rate of growth of output per worker by three-digit industries, 1960–81 (percentages)*

Industrial code	Industry major group	1960-65	1966-70	1960-70	1971-75	1976-81	1971-81	1960-81
311-2	Food	8.3	16.2	11.4	12.9	8.9	10.9	10.5
313	Beverages	1.2	-0.1	1.8	13.5	15.9	14.9	8.0
314	Cigarettes and other tobacco products	9.5	8.7	8.7	4.6	8.8	7.9	7.9
321	Textiles and textile manufactures				12.0	11.5	13.9	
322	Wearing apparel except footwear	-7.8	5.5	-1.3	14.7	11.1	13.7	13.5
323	Leather and leather products				8.5	5.4	8.6	
324	Footwear				10.2	14.6	13.6	
331	Sawn timber and other wood products except furniture	–	8.2	3.6	15.7	10.0	15.4	8.4
332	Furniture and fixtures except primarily of metal	4.9	1.4	4.2	6.6	15.1	11.4	7.7
341	Paper and paper products	1.0	2.7	2.2	14.9	16.2	15.1	8.6
342	Printing and publishing	4.8	0.5	2.9	13.4	11.0	12.9	8.1
351	Industrial chemicals and gases			–	22.3	5.5	14.3	
352	Paints, pharmaceutical and other chemical products	21.2	15.9	17.4	27.5	11.6	18.2	24.5
353-4	Petroleum refineries and petroleum products				23.4	16.3	20.9	
355	Processing of jelutong and gum damar	-4.9[1]	11.7[1]	3.4	14.1	12.5	11.9	12.3
356	Rubber products except rubber footwear				9.3	7.5	8.0	
357	Plastic products				12.4	13.6	14.1	
361-2	Pottery, china, earthenware and glass products	–	–	–	30.0	11.2	18.6	
363	Bricks, tiles and other structural clay products				15.7	27.6	21.1	
364	Cement and cement additives	17.1	2.6	9.8	30.1	21.3	22.4	27.2
365	Structural cement and concrete products				20.9	21.7	20.8	
369	Asbestos, stone and other non-metallic mineral products				16.7	17.5	14.7	
371	Iron and steel	19.4	14.9	17.0	22.7	12.3	14.7	19.8
372	Zinc and other non-ferrous metals				23.4	3.6	21.9	
381	Metal grills, cans, pipes and other fabricated products	4.9	1.4	3.6	16.3	12.4	12.1	7.3
382	Calculators, refrigerators, air-conditioners and industrial machinery	4.3	8.2	5.4	24.5	19.5	17.4	11.0
383	Radios, televisions, semi-conductors and other electrical machinery	5.0	0.1	4.3	19.1	11.7	14.0	8.7
384	Transport equipment and oil rigs	-0.4	7.6	3.9	20.3	11.2	14.1	8.5
385	Professional and scientific equipment and photographic and optical goods			–	7.2	15.4	10.4	–
390	Other manufacturing industries (jewellery, toys, umbrellas, etc.)	2.1[2]	-9.4[2]	-2.0	21.2	13.7	16.5	6.9
	Total manufacturing excluding rubber processing	6.2	6.5	6.6	18.5	12.1	14.6	10.2

Sources and notes: Same as table 9.

Table 28. Value-added to output by three-digit industries, 1960-81 (percentages)

Industrial code	Industry major group	1960	1965	1970	1975	1980	1981
311-2	Food	22.2	20.7	13.9	17.8	15.7	21.0
313	Beverages	50.1	56.1	52.5	43.8	43.8	42.8
314	Cigarettes and other tobacco products	19.9	33.5	25.4	24.0	30.7	35.2
321	Textiles and textile manufactures			27.9	30.3	32.2	32.0
322	Wearing apparel except footwear	29.2	27.1	27.7	32.2	31.4	33.3
323	Leather and leather products			17.4	20.9	28.6	27.3
324	Footwear			35.5	38.4	35.8	34.6
331	Sawn timber and other wood products except furniture	28.2	29.5	32.4	25.9	24.1	27.4
332	Furniture and fixtures except primarily of metal	35.2	46.3	44.4	44.0	37.1	36.9
341	Paper and paper products	36.4	35.9	33.0	32.8	34.6	34.3
342	Printing and publishing	57.4	56.3	51.9	55.5	50.5	50.7
351	Industrial chemicals and gases			45.9	30.0	31.6	32.8
352	Paints, pharmaceutical and other chemical products	15.3	22.8	43.1	50.0	52.1	51.4
353-4	Petroleum refineries and petroleum products			17.2	12.7	12.8	11.8
355	Processing of jelutong and gum damar	18.3 [1]	34.3 [1]	11.1	12.5	11.1	13.1
356	Rubber products except rubber footwear			47.9	45.7	43.7	44.9
357	Plastic products	–	–	32.9	32.3	34.9	35.6
361-2	Pottery, china, earthenware and glass products			55.2	41.6	36.1	40.7
363	Bricks, tiles and other structural clay products			71.0	61.5	61.2	60.0
364	Cement and cement additives	31.6	46.2	21.0	28.7	17.6	22.6
365	Structural cement and concrete products			31.7	32.5	34.3	29.6
369	Asbestos, stone and other non-metallic mineral products			38.5	41.8	46.0	45.0
371	Iron and steel	38.7	40.8	33.9	34.5	39.0	40.3
372	Zinc and other non-ferrous metals			20.2	27.2	11.5	19.4
381	Metal grills, cans, pipes and other fabricated products	35.8	31.4	33.0	34.3	33.7	36.0
382	Calculators, refrigerators, air-conditioners and industrial machinery	38.8	43.4	37.9	45.9	44.8	45.9
383	Radios, televisions, semi-conductors and other electrical machinery	46.1	43.7	45.0	31.7	32.1	29.7
384	Transport equipment and oil rigs	26.2	38.7	48.3	46.4	51.9	53.1
385	Professional and scientific equipment and photographic and optical goods	–	–	28.1	48.2	45.0	38.0
390	Other manufacturing industries (jewellery, toys, umbrellas, etc.)	18.9 [2]	23.4 [2]	24.3	24.8	29.1	28.3
	Total manufacturing excluding rubber processing	30.5	32.1	28.1	27.1	26.9	26.4

[1] Includes rubber footwear.   [2] Includes plastic products.

Sources: Singapore, Department of Statistics: *Report on the Census of Industrial Production, 1960/61* (Singapore, Government Printing Office, 1964), p. 24; idem: *Report on the Census of Industrial Production, 1965* (Singapore, Government Printing Office, 1966), p. 19; idem: *Report on the Census of Industrial Production, 1981* (Singapore, Namic Printers Pte Ltd., 1982), pp. 28-29.

Table 29.   Capital expenditure per worker by three-digit industries, 1960-81 (S$'000)

Industrial code	Industry major group	1960	1965	1970	1975	1980	1981
311-2	Food	0.4	1.5	2.0	2.8	6.6	8.3
313	Beverages	0.6	0.3	1.2	2.1	5.2	5.8
314	Cigarettes and other tobacco products	1.5	1.2	0.9	2.2	8.3	4.0
321	Textiles and textile manufactures			3.7	3.3	5.6	3.4
322	Wearing apparel except footwear	0.1	0.6	0.6	0.5	1.2	1.3
323	Leather and leather products			0.2	0.3	1.2	1.0
324	Footwear			0.5	0.4	3.4	4.1
331	Sawn timber and other wood products except furniture	0.1	1.0	2.1	1.0	2.9	3.5
332	Furniture and fixtures except primarily of metal	0.1	0.4	0.7	0.9	2.2	2.4
341	Paper and paper products	0.1	1.8	1.3	1.7	9.1	20.0
342	Printing and publishing	0.4	1.1	3.7	2.2	3.8	7.4
351	Industrial chemicals and gases			14.1	7.1	18.9	42.4
352	Paints, pharmaceutical and other chemical products	0.3	4.8	1.8	5.4	6.2	8.6
353-4	Petroleum refineries and petroleum products			74.4	29.7	158.4	107.2
355	Processing of jelutong and gum damar	0.3 [1]	1.1 [1]	0.8	2.5	0.3	1.0
356	Rubber products except rubber footwear			2.5	1.5	1.7	4.0
357	Plastic products	–	–	2.1	2.9	4.4	6.0
361-2	Pottery, china, earthenware and glass products			1.6	0.4	30.5	4.8
363	Bricks, tiles and other structural clay products			1.8	1.9	9.6	7.7
364	Cement and cement additives	0.5	0.6	17.0	41.3	5.5	7.3
365	Structural cement and concrete products			3.2	4.7	5.3	10.5
369	Asbestos, stone and other non-metallic mineral products			0.9	3.1	2.3	5.8
371	Iron and steel	0.2	2.3	5.0	9.7	9.3	6.7
372	Zinc and other non-ferrous metals			2.6	1.6	10.3	23.6
381	Metal grills, cans, pipes and other fabricated products	0.4	0.9	2.0	1.9	8.7	7.8
382	Calculators, refrigerators, air-conditioners and industrial machinery	0.1	1.5	2.4	6.2	7.3	0.9
383	Radios, televisions, semi-conductors and other electrical machinery	0.3	0.6	2.8	2.2	3.9	4.7
384	Transport equipment and oil rigs	0.2	1.8	2.0	3.0	5.5	0.4
385	Professional and scientific equipment and photographic and optical goods	–	–	0.7	4.6	3.6	5.8
390	Other manufacturing industries (jewellery, toys, umbrellas, etc.)	0.04 [2]	1.2 [2]	1.0	1.4	3.1	3.0
	Total manufacturing excluding rubber processing	0.4	1.3	3.5	3.3	6.5	7.0

[1] Includes rubber footwear.   [2] Includes plastic products.

Sources: Singapore, Department of Statistics: *Report on the Census of Industrial Production, 1960/61* (Singapore, Government Printing Office, 1964), p. 24; idem: *Report on the Census of Industrial Production, 1965* (Singapore, Government Printing Office, 1966), p. 19; idem: *Report on the Census of Industrial Production, 1980* (Singapore, Singapore National Printers, 1981), pp. 30-31; idem: *Report on the Census of Industrial Production, 1981* (Singapore, Namic Printers Pte Ltd., 1982), pp. 30-31.

Table 30. **Capital expenditure to output by three-digit industries, 1960-81 (percentages)**

Industrial code	Industry major group	1960	1965	1970	1975	1980	1981
311-2	Food	2.0	4.7	3.2	2.9	4.0	4.9
313	Beverages	2.3	1.4	4.2	4.3	5.5	4.9
314	Cigarettes and other tobacco products	3.8	1.8	0.9	2.0	6.2	2.0
321	Textiles and textile manufactures			31.0	14.4	11.2	6.4
322	Wearing apparel except footwear	1.2	7.1	7.5	3.1	4.0	3.8
323	Leather and leather products			0.9	1.3	3.2	2.3
324	Footwear			5.9	2.8	9.8	10.6
331	Sawn timber and other wood products except furniture	0.4	6.8	10.6	2.9	4.0	4.5
332	Furniture and fixtures except primarily of metal	1.1	3.9	5.0	4.6	6.0	5.8
341	Paper and paper products	1.0	14.9	8.9	5.8	14.3	29.8
342	Printing and publishing	4.1	8.2	26.7	8.2	8.3	13.7
351	Industrial chemicals and gases			32.8	7.2	11.7	24.0
352	Paints, pharmaceutical and other chemical products	0.8	4.1	7.2	7.1	4.5	5.6
353-4	Petroleum refineries and petroleum products			13.4	2.1	4.6	2.6
355	Processing of jelutong and gum damar	1.5 [1]	6.9 [1]	1.4	2.6	0.2	0.5
356	Rubber products except rubber footwear			10.5	4.2	3.6	7.4
357	Plastic products	–	–	13.0	10.8	8.1	10.6
361-2	Pottery, china, earthenware and glass products			16.3	0.9	42.9	6.0
363	Bricks, tiles and other structural clay products			24.6	9.4	14.9	10.1
364	Cement and cement additives	6.6	3.6	20.2	15.2	0.9	1.0
365	Structural cement and concrete products			17.5	9.5	4.9	6.9
369	Asbestos, stone and other non-metallic mineral products			4.4	6.0	2.6	5.3
371	Iron and steel	1.5	9.0	10.7	9.4	5.2	3.7
372	Zinc and other non-ferrous metals			4.3	1.8	2.5	8.1
381	Metal grills, cans, pipes and other fabricated products	2.5	4.1	7.9	4.2	12.5	10.2
382	Calculators, refrigerators, air-conditioners and industrial machinery	1.3	10.4	12.0	13.0	8.8	8.7
383	Radios, televisions, semi-conductors and other electrical machinery	1.8	3.6	13.3	5.2	5.2	6.0
384	Transport equipment and oil rigs	1.5	13.5	9.7	6.8	7.4	5.4
385	Professional and scientific equipment and photographic and optical goods	–	–	4.9	17.5	9.8	10.9
390	Other manufacturing industries (jewellery, toys, umbrellas, etc.)	0.2 [2]	5.9 [2]	7.0	4.0	4.9	4.0
	Total manufacturing excluding rubber processing	2.1	5.5	10.8	4.9	5.9	5.3

[1] Includes rubber footwear. [2] Includes plastic products.

Sources: Singapore, Department of Statistics: *Report on the Census of Industrial Production, 1960/61* (Singapore, Government Printing Office, 1964), p. 24; idem: *Report on the Census of Industrial Production, 1965* (Singapore, Government Printing Office, 1966), p. 19; idem: *Report on the Census of Industrial Production, 1980* (Singapore, Singapore National Printers, 1981), pp. 30-31; idem: *Report on the Census of Industrial Production, 1981* (Singapore, Namic Printers Pte Ltd., 1982), pp. 30-31.

Summary and evaluation

These first two chapters have outlined and detailed Singapore's economic progress over the past two decades. GDP has grown very rapidly and the structure of the economy has changed from one based on entrepot trade and services to one based on export manufacturing, finance, transport and communications. Economically, there is no doubt that Singapore has done very well, given its limited resource base and small domestic market. Labour is the country's main resource, and it has been fully employed since the early 1970s. In fact, a persistent domestic labour shortage has necessitated the importation of large numbers of temporary and permanent foreign workers (see Chapter 3).

Singapore's domestic labour resources have been underutilised in predominantly low-skill, low-value, low-wage, labour-intensive activities, such as those found in most of the export manufacturing industries. Because of this, labour has probably benefited less from economic growth than capital, and its share of national income has remained at less than half. But at the same time the mass creation of jobs has improved the personal income distribution.[5]

The costs of rapid economic growth in Singapore lie more in the social and political than in the economic realm. For example, the rush to provide mass education at a level suitable for low-skilled employment in labour-intensive factories has led until recent reforms to a relative neglect of quality in the school system, resulting in a low level of general educational attainment. The need to ensure political stability in order to attract foreign investment required constraints on political freedoms. These constraints have diminished in recent years with increasing liberalisation. Rapid urban renewal and housing resettlement have led to the destruction of historical areas, and the breaking up of extended families and established communities. Here too greater attempts are now being made by the Government to preserve historical sites, to foster the three-generation family unit and a renewed community spirit or "neighbourliness".

Rapid economic and population growth have led to greater physical and traffic congestion and highlighted the improving but still inadequate public transport system. The pressures of living in a rapidly changing and highly competitive urban society have also resulted in an increasing incidence of social problems such as family discord, mental and psychological problems among adults and schoolchildren, suicide, child neglect and abuse, and so on. However, these problems are not any different from, and most probably less serious than those in many other rapidly industrialising societies.

Certainly, these costs of rapid development in Singapore's tightly run society are minor and do not outweigh the material benefits to the population, which has secure jobs, adequate and rising incomes, homes, educational opportunities for their children, and good health facilities. The accompanying state interventions in personal choices – for example, of how many children to have, where to live, where to go to school, and what to study in school and university, etc., are increasingly influenced by government rules and incentives – are widely regarded as necessary for social order and progress.

For continued economic progress, Singapore needs to upgrade its economic activities, especially its manufacturing sector, and to maximise utilisation of its domestic labour force. Investment and manpower policies have already been enacted to effect this (see Chapter 3). At the same time, an increasingly educated and ambitious citizenry is likely to demand more individual choices and greater popular participation in politics and in economic decision-making. The challenge to the Government in the 1980s is to meet these demands and still maintain the social stability and discipline that make sustained economic growth possible.

Notes

[1] "Highlights of Singapore's Economic Development Plan for the Eighties", Appendix I of *Towards higher achievement*, Budget speech 1981 by Goh Chok Tong, Minister for Trade and Industry (March 1981).

[2] ibid.

[3] For a full list of the various incentives for manufacturing and servicing activities, see Singapore International Chamber of Commerce: *Investor's guide to the economic climate of Singapore* (Singapore, SICC, July 1981), pp. 21-30.

[4] The full list of priority industries is given in Appendix A. Appendix B gives examples of major international companies operating in Singapore.

[5] Pang Eng Fong: "Growth, inequality and race in Singapore", in *International Labour Review* (Geneva, ILO), Jan. 1975, pp. 15-28.

Appendix A

List of "priority" industries Singapore is promoting in the 1980s

Electrical/electronics

Computers and peripheral equipment and software development.
Instrumentation and industrial controls.
Telecommunication equipment.
Advanced electronic components including semiconductor wafer fabrication and silicone crystal growing.
Power generation and distribution equipment.
Electrical motors and switchgear.
High value home appliances.
Solar cells and optical fibres.

Machinery and precision engineering

Conventional, NC/CNC and other precision machine tools and accessories, metal cutting and metal forming machinery, tools and dies.
Photographic and optical instruments, e.g. cameras, microscopes, spectographs.
Medical instruments and devices, e.g. surgical instruments, dental equipment, diagnostic and patient monitoring apparatus, prosthetic devices.
Office equipment, e.g. copiers, electronic typewriters, cash registers, facsimile.
Precision measuring tools, e.g. micrometers, comparators and components, e.g. hydraulic/pneumatic valves, sensors and transducers.
Industrial machinery and components, e.g. plastic fabrication machinery, woodworking and textile machinery, robotics.

Transport equipment and heavy/basic metal engineering

Oilfield equipment and services.
Aircraft components, e.g. hydraulic flight control equipment, fuel pumps, avionics.
Automotive components, e.g. transmission, clutch, brake assemblies, carburettors, automotive electronics.
Industrial process plant fabrication, pumps, compressors, valves.
Ship machinery and equipment.
Special steels, forging, investment casting, precision sheet metal and other supporting industries.
Diesel engines, turbines and related components.
Mining, construction and agricultural equipment, and related components.

Petroleum/chemicals/petrochemicals/plastics

Specialty industrial chemicals.
Fine chemicals.
Pharmaceuticals.
Engineering plastics.

Appendix B

List of some international companies operating in Singapore

Chemical process industries

Amoco, British Petroleum, Esso, Mobil, Shell (refined petroleum products); Denki Kagaku Kogyo (acetylene black); Phillips Petroleum (high density polyethylene); Sumitomo Chemical (low density polyethylene and propylene); BP Chemicals (phenolic and epoxy laminates; Exxon Chemicals (lube oil additives); Dyno (industrial chemicals); Mitsui (formalin, plywood adhesives); Union Carbide (polyvinylacetates); Sumitomo (PVC resins and compounds); ICI, Nippon Paint, Kansai Paint, Jotungrappen (paints); Collie, Dainippon Ink & Chemicals (printing inks); Kowa (activated carbon); Kiwi (polishes); Singapore Oxygen Air Liquids (industrial and medical gases); Albright & Wilson (detergent intermediate chemicals); Beecham (semi-synthetic penicillins); Glaxo (proprietary drugs); Drug Houses of Australia (pharmaceuticals); Kanegafuchi (amino acids); Beecham, Wella, Shiseido, Tancho (cosmetics); Unilever (detergents and toiletries); Economics Laboratory (detergents); Petrolite (demulsifiers); Dunlop (foam-rubber products); Betz (water treatment chemicals); Mitsubishi (V-belts); Tigers Polymer (plastic hoses and moulded products); Dai-Ichi Seiko (engineering plastics); Showa Plastics, Showa Denko Diamond Plastics (plastic mouldings); Beatrice (dairy products); Tetra Pak (laminated packaging materials).

Food and beverages

Beecham, Wander (food beverages); Nestlé (dairy and culinary products, malt extract); McCormick & Stange (oleoresins); Nissin Foods (instant and cup noodles); Moija Seika (confectionery); Zuellig (animal feed).

Precision engineering

Daini-Seikosha and Suwa Seikosha (wrist watches); LeBlond (engine lathes and iron castings); Okamoto (precision surface grinders); Smith-Corona (portable electric typewriters); Normalair-Garrett (precision investment casting); SKF (ball and roller bearings); Timex (precision tools and dies, watch components); Hilgeland (cold-heading machinery); Fujitec Co. (elevators); Pelmec (ball bearings); NMB (miniature ball bearings, stepper motors and printer calculators); Shimano (bicycle gears); Vollmer (saw doctoring machines); Incom (precision roller chains and marine cables); Traub (automatic lathes); Schmidtmann (woodworking machinery); Leeds & Northrup (thermocouples); California Pellet Mills (pellet mills); Tata (precision tools and dies); Mustad Industries (fish hooks); Papenmeier (plastic processing machinery); Japan Steel Works (injection moulding machines); Nachi-Fujikoshi (cutting tools); Bridgeport (milling machines); Walbro (non-automative carburettors); Hitachi Koki (electric power tools); SSIH/NMB (watch cases); Dorma (door closers); Dynacast (zinc precision diecast); Baumann (precision springs); Buckbee Mears (IC lead frames); Precision Valve Corp. (aerosol valves); Sandvik (saws and drills); Casomold (precision tools); Festo (pneumatic valves and cylinders); Azumi (gear hobs); Hitachi Powdered Metals (powder metallurgy products, toolings); Matsushita Technical Centre (toolings); Johns Consolidated (injection moulding machine components); LVD (press brakes, guillotine shears); Netstal (injection moulding machines); OMCO (glass moulds).

Oilfield equipment, shipbuilding and repairing

Cameron Iron Works (oilfield equipment and valves); Hydril (drill pipes); Baker Oil Tools (speciality oilfield equipment); Hughes Tool (tool joints); Van Der Horst (porous chrome plating); FMC (wellhead equipment); Vetco (wellhead equipment); Tri-State (oilfield fishing tools, casing connectors); National Supply (wellheads); Eastman Whipstock (directional survey equipment); Baker Marine (jack up systems, cranes and winches); TRW Reda Pump (electric submersible pumps); Stone Manganese Marine (ship propellors and shafts); local shipyards (barges, tugs, fast naval crafts, supply vessels, LASH and Ro-Ro vessels, bulk carriers, LPG and chemical carriers); Jurong Shipyard (freighters, 86,000 dwt. oil tankers); Bethlehem, Far East Levingston, Marathon LeTourneau, Robin, Promet (semi-submersible oil-rigs, jackups, drillships); Hitachi, Keppel, Mitsubishi; Sembawang, Jurong Shipyard (comprehensive repair facilities for vessels up to 400,000 dwt.).

Engineering consultancy services

Brown & Root, McDermott Engineering, RJ Brown & Associates, Protech, Chiyoda Engineering, Matthew Hall Engineering, Pilkenrood Vinitex.

Electronics

Fairchild (integrated circuits); GE (electron tubes, motors, household appliances and components, CTV sub-assemblies, TV components); Fujitsu (crossbar exchange equipment and mercury relays); Philips (telecom equipment, consumer electronic products); Hewlett-Packard (programmable calculators, oscilloscopes); Matsushita (refrigerator compressors, consumer electronic products, semiconductors and other electronic components, micromotors); Sanyo (consumer electronic products and domestic appliances); Hitachi (consumer electrical and electronic appliances); Sumitomo Electric (enamelled wires); Karl Hopt (capacitors and resistors); SGS-Ates (semiconductors); National Semiconductor (semi-conductors); Siemens (semiconductors, opto-electronic tubes, lasers, liquid crystal displays, electrolytic capacitors); NMB (hi-fi equipment, printing calculators); Thomson-Brandt (consumer electronic products, household appliance components); General Motors (car radio/stereos); Mitsubishi Electric (B/W TV picture tubes, B/W tubes, B/W TV sets); Nippon Electric (digital fluorescent display tubes); Aiwa (radios and cassette tape recorders); Hy-Q (quartz crystals); Synertek Inc. (semiconductors, autofocusing modules); CTS (resistors, switches); Nichicon (capacitors); Okaya Electric (capacitors, neon glow lamps); Digital Equipment Corp. (computer equipment and parts); DuPont (connectors); Foxboro (process control instrumentation); Molex (connectors); Texas Instruments (semi-conductors, tools and dies); Veeco (switching power supplies); Demetron (printed circuit boards, IC bonding wires); Olivetti (printing calculators); Thomson-SCF (semiconductor testing); Data Recording Heads, Woelke (magnetic heads); JVC Trio Kenwood (high-fidelity equipment); Apple Computer (micro-computer equipment and parts); Micro Peripheral Inc. (floppy disc drives); Hindustan Computers (small business computers).

Electrical

Brown Boveri & Cie (mini-circuit breakers); ASEA (industrial and marine switchboards); Telemecanique (busbar trunking); Westinghouse Electric, Australasia (motor and industrial electrical equipment servicing); Electrical Equipment of Australia-GMF (grinders); Yokogawa (measuring instruments); Union Carbide (dry cell batteries); GEC (household electrical appliances); Varta (Ni-Cd batteries); Copal (digital clock movements and cassette mechanisms); Sumitomo Electric (enamelled wires); Elektrisk Bureau (communication equipment); Crompton Parkinson (electrical measuring instruments); MEM (miniature circuit breakers); Meiden (distribution transformers); Reyrolle Parsons (LV and HV switchgears); Tamco Cutler-Hammer (electrical control equipment); Teco (electrical motors); Sumiden (enamelled wires); MK (electrical acessories); Merlin Gerlin (LV switchgear).

Precision optics

United Scientific Holdings (optical instruments and components); Wild (scientific optical instruments); FJW (optical elements); Polycore (hard resin ophthalmic lenses); Sola Optical (plastic ophthalmic lenses); Balzers (multi-layer lens coating); NEC (motion analysis instruments).

Aerospace

Sundstrand (aerospace components and devices); Garett AiResearch (TPE and APU overhaul and aircraft components); GE (aero-engine components); Interturbine (refurbishing of aircraft hot sections); Parker Hannifin (hydraulic flight control system); Aerospatiale (helicopters).

Medical

Baxter Travenol (kidney dialysis plates); Japan Medical Supply (administration sets, blood bags); Gallus (dental chairs); Meditec (hearing aids); Taksuki (disposable syringes and hypodermic needles).

Chapter 3

The dynamics of development

Enterprises

Singapore's economy is built by private enterprise, both indigenous and foreign. Since the colonial era there has been a dualistic industrial structure, comprising large foreign corporate enterprises on the one hand, and a large number of small, highly competitive local enterprises – many of them family businesses – on the other. Both were involved largely in commercial and service activities, with manufacturing becoming important only from the late 1960s. The following discussion will focus on the manufacturing sector.

Both the foreign and indigenous business communities are dynamic and active in search of profit opportunities reflecting world as well as local market forces. The foreign business community, originally dominated by British commercial enterprises, has since independence become increasingly diversified by nationality and by business activity. It now includes significant numbers of other Europeans, citizens of the United States and Japan, and other Asians, the latter mainly Chinese from Hong Kong, Malaysia and Indonesia and elsewhere. While the Europeans, Americans and Japanese are concentrated largely but not exclusively in large enterprises, especially subsidiaries of multinational corporations, the other Asians operate on a smaller scale, frequently in joint ventures with indigenous entrepreneurs, who are also mainly ethnic Chinese.

While the local and overseas Chinese business communities comprise mostly individual entrepreneurs, small businessmen and operators of family businesses, members of the foreign business community are mostly corporate employees who manage rather than own the enterprises they work for. Non-Singapore citizens account for nearly one in five of all administrative and managerial personnel in Singapore.[1] Foreign and local managers employed in foreign subsidiaries respond not only to the Government's development strategy but also to the global interests of parent companies. Thus they often merely execute investment and management policies dictated by foreign headquarters, rather than exercise full local initiative.

Local entrepreneurship is abundantly available from diverse sources. Some local entrepreneurs have branched into manufacturing from traditional family businesses in the commercial sector, often in response to the profit opportunities provided by a tariff-protected domestic market. Others have set up their own businesses after acquiring some technical or marketing experience as employees, often in large foreign firms.[2] The desire and ability to set up in business for oneself is seen as being "in the blood" of a recently immigrant population, and has been identified as one cause of high employee turnover and "lack of company loyalty" among industrial managers and professionals.

As table 31 shows, the private limited liability company is the most common form of legal organisation for manufacturing enterprises. In 1981 such companies accounted for nearly 90 per cent of all manufacturing output, 94 per cent of manufactured exports, and 83 per cent of manufacturing employment, having increased their share of all these since 1975. There were many sole proprietorships and partnerships, but their share of output, exports and employment was small. Although there were relatively few public limited liability companies, they had the largest mean size of output and employment.

Table 32 shows the increasing dominance of foreign enterprises in the manufacturing sector, and their large size relative to local enterprises. Whereas wholly and majority foreign-owned enterprises accounted for more than a quarter of all manufacturing enterprises in 1981, they produced three-quarters of the output and 87 per cent of the direct exports, and employed 59 per cent of the workers in this sector. Wholly foreign-owned firms had the largest mean output, employment and capital expenditure per establishment, and the highest value-added per worker, while wholly local firms ranked lowest by all these criteria. The local firms also produced mainly for the local market, while the foreign firms exported more than three-quarters of their output. Since the mid-1970s both foreign and local firms have shown a trend towards stable or declining employment size per firm,[3] with greater export orientation, more capital expenditure, and higher value-added per worker. This reflects the market-induced upgrading of manufacturing industry in advance of the "Second Industrial Revolution" policies announced by the Government in 1979.

Table 33 shows the relative weight of investors of different nationalities in the manufacturing sector. Singapore firms account for the largest number and share of establishments (74 per cent), workers (42 per cent), and total output (34 per cent) in this sector, and rank second in terms of export (23.6 per cent of the total). But they are the smallest firms in terms of average employment size (46 workers) and second smallest in output (S$4.9 million) per establishment, and rank lowest in terms of average capital expenditure, and the percentage of output exported (42 per cent). Though they are small, labour-intensive and oriented largely towards the domestic market, they surpass the larger, export-oriented firms from Japan, Hong Kong and the Federal Republic of Germany in terms of value-added per worker.

Other European firms rank first in average output size, capital expenditure and value-added per worker, and rank second in terms of output (25 per cent) and export (32 per cent) share, average employment size (283) and percentage of output exported (79 per cent). Their high ranking reflects the heavy investment by other European nationalities, especially the Dutch, in the large-scale, capital-intensive, high value-added, petroleum refining industry which is the manufacturing sector's largest in terms of assets, output and exports. Firms from the United States rank largest in average employment size (363), second in average output and capital expenditure, and third in number of establishments, number of employees and value-added per worker. They dominate

Table 31. *Principal statistics of manufacturing by legal organisation, 1975-81*

Legal status of establishment	Number of establishments		Number of workers		Output		Average output per establishment	Value-added		Direct imports		Capital expenditure	
	No.	%	No.	%	S$m	%	S$ ('000)	S$m	%	S$m	%	S$m	%
1975													
Total	2 385	100.0	191 528	100.0	12 610.1	100.0	5 287.3	3 411.1	100.0	7 200.7	100.0	622.6	100.0
Sole proprietorship	429	18.0	8 839	4.6	177.4	1.4	413.4	58.2	1.7	19.9	0.3	4.9	0.8
Partnership	570	23.9	11 635	6.1	265.9	2.1	466.5	85.6	2.5	25.8	0.4	7.7	1.2
Public limited liability company	74	3.1	30 151	15.7	1 471.9	11.7	19 890.1	578.5	17.0	598.2	8.3	86.1	13.8
Private limited liability company	1 307	54.8	140 500	73.4	10 667.3	84.6	8 161.6	2 671.0	78.3	6 538.1	90.8	522.1	83.8
Others	5	0.2	403	0.2	27.8	0.2	5 554.8	17.7	0.5	18.7	0.3	1.8	0.3
1980													
Total	3 355	100.0	285 250	100.0	31 657.9	100.0	9 436.0	8 521.9	100.0	19 172.9	100.0	1 861.9	100.0
Sole proprietorship	414	12.3	7 244	2.5	261.3	0.8	631.2	80.1	0.9	27.7	0.1	10.2	0.5
Partnership	653	19.5	12 097	4.2	438.4	1.4	671.4	138.8	1.6	42.8	0.2	18.1	1.0
Public limited liability company	65	1.9	26 184	9.2	2 511.9	7.9	38 644.9	1 005.7	11.8	1 048.2	5.5	143.4	7.7
Private limited liability company	2 207	65.8	238 574	83.6	28 297.1	89.4	12 821.5	7 233.0	84.9	17 966.3	93.7	1 678.7	90.2
Others	16	0.5	1 151	0.4	149.1	0.5	9 321.1	64.3	0.8	87.9	0.5	11.4	0.6
1981													
Total	3 439	100.0	281 675	100.0	36 787.1	100.0	10 697.0	9 720.5	100.0	22 375.3	100.0	1 966.8	100.0
Sole proprietorship	423	12.3	7 069	2.5	293.8	0.8	694.5	91.8	0.9	19.5	0.1	14.3	0.7
Partnership	620	18.0	11 369	4.0	466.8	1.3	753.0	154.7	1.6	47.2	0.2	17.6	0.9
Public limited liability company	67	1.9	28 120	10.0	2 928.1	8.0	43 703.3	1 207.9	12.4	1 196.1	5.3	155.2	7.9
Private limited liability company	2 307	67.1	233 023	82.7	32 875.8	89.4	14 250.4	8 148.3	83.8	20 978.0	93.8	1 747.4	88.8
Others	22	0.6	2 094	0.7	222.6	0.6	10 118.6	117.9	1.2	134.4	0.6	32.2	1.6

Sources: Singapore, Department of Statistics: *Report on the Census of Industrial Production, 1975* (Singapore, Photoplates Private Ltd., 1976), p. 16; idem: *Report on the Census of Industrial Production, 1980* (Singapore, Singapore National Printers, 1981), p. 4; idem: *Report on the Census of Industrial Production, 1981* (Singapore, Namic Printers Pte Ltd., 1982), p. 4.

Table 32. Principal statistics of manufacturing by capital structure, 1975-81

Legal status of establishment	Number of establishments		Number of workers		Output		Value-added		Direct exports		Capital expenditure		Average output per establishment	Average employment per establishment	Average expenditure per establishment	Average value-added per worker	Average proportion of output exported
	No.	%	No.	%	S$m	%	S$m	%	S$m	%	S$m	%	S$'000	No.	S$'000	S$'000	%
1975																	
Total	2 385	100.0	191 528	100.0	12 610.1	100.0	3 411.1	100.0	7 200.7	100.0	622.6	100.0	5 287.3	80	261.0	17.8	57.1
Wholly local	1 595	66.9	62 903	32.8	2 276.5	18.0	828.4	24.3	641.8	8.9	129.0	20.7	1 427.2	39	80.9	13.2	28.2
Majority local	265	11.1	29 038	15.2	1 346.2	10.7	444.3	13.0	500.6	7.0	91.3	14.7	5 080.1	110	344.4	15.3	37.2
Minority local	228	9.6	39 211	20.5	1 901.5	15.1	521.4	15.3	1 295.6	18.0	108.7	17.5	8 339.8	172	476.6	13.3	68.1
Wholly foreign	297	12.5	60 376	31.5	7 086.0	56.2	1 617.1	47.4	4 762.7	66.1	293.1	47.2	23 858.6	203	989.0	26.8	67.2
1980																	
Total	3 355	100.0	285 250	100.0	31 657.9	100.0	8 521.9	100.0	19 172.9	100.0	1 861.9	100.0	9 436.0	85	555.0	29.9	60.6
Wholly local	2 153	64.2	80 262	28.1	4 943.6	15.6	1 624.2	19.1	1 357.3	7.1	264.3	14.2	2 296.1	37	122.8	20.2	27.5
Majority local	368	11.0	38 329	13.4	3 385.1	10.7	1 154.1	13.5	1 573.5	8.2	208.9	11.2	9 198.8	104	567.7	30.1	46.5
Minority local	318	9.5	52 861	18.5	4 736.8	15.0	1 133.2	13.3	2 535.7	13.2	246.8	13.3	14 895.6	166	776.2	21.4	53.5
Wholly foreign	516	15.4	113 798	39.9	18 592.4	58.7	4 610.3	54.1	13 706.3	71.5	1 141.8	61.3	36 031.8	221	2 212.8	40.5	73.7
1981																	
Total	3 439	100.0	281 675	100.0	36 787.1	100.0	9 720.5	100.0	22 375.3	100.0	1 966.8	100.0	10 697.0	82	571.9	34.5	60.8
Wholly local	2 177	63.3	79 778	28.3	5 309.9	14.4	1 865.8	19.2	1 394.5	6.2	337.3	17.1	2 439.1	37	154.9	23.4	26.3
Majority local	363	10.6	37 229	13.2	3 515.1	9.6	1 274.3	13.1	1 563.2	7.0	217.9	11.1	9 683.4	103	600.2	34.2	44.5
Minority local	323	9.4	44 101	15.7	7 409.4	20.1	1 301.8	13.4	4 430.4	19.8	188.5	9.6	22 939.2	137	583.6	29.5	59.8
Wholly foreign	576	16.7	120 567	42.8	20 552.8	55.9	5 278.6	54.3	14 987.2	67.0	1 223.1	62.2	35 681.9	209	2 123.4	43.8	72.9

Sources: Singapore, Department of Statistics: *Report on the Census of Industrial Production, 1975* (Singapore, Photoplates Private Ltd., 1976), p. 16; idem: *Report on the Census of Industrial Production, 1980* (Singapore, Singapore National Printers, 1981), p. 4; idem: *Report on the Census of Industrial Production, 1981* (Singapore, Namic Printers Pte Ltd., 1982), p. 4.

Table 33. Principal statistics of manufacturing by major source of capital, 1981

Major source of capital	Number of establishments		Number of workers		Output		Value-added		Direct exports		Capital expenditure		Average output per establishment	Average employment per establishment	Average expenditure per establishment	Average value-added per worker	Average proportion of output exported
	No.	%	No.	%	S$m	%	S$m	%	S$m	%	S$m	%	S$'000	No.	S$'000	S$'000	%
Total	3 439	100.0	281 675	100.0	36 787.1	100.0	9 720.5	100.0	22 375.3	100.0	1 966.8	100.0	10 697.0	82	571.9	34.5	60.8
Singapore	2 556	74.3	118 780	42.2	12 564.1	34.2	3 264.1	33.6	5 288.3	23.6	566.9	28.8	4 915.5	46	221.8	27.5	42.1
Australia	47	1.4	3 411	1.2	230.8	0.6	105.6	1.1	106.2	0.5	21.0	1.1	4 910.5	73	447.6	31.0	46.0
Hong Kong	88	2.6	14 437	5.1	1 039.3	2.8	305.6	3.1	828.4	3.7	124.9	6.3	11 810.6	164	1 418.8	21.2	79.7
Japan	186	5.4	45 218	16.1	3 348.0	9.1	1 024.7	10.5	2 226.9	10.0	244.9	12.5	18 000.2	243	1 316.6	22.7	66.5
Malaysia	77	2.2	5 362	1.9	607.9	1.7	251.4	2.6	261.1	1.2	44.1	2.2	7 894.7	70	572.9	46.9	43.0
Switzerland	25	0.7	5 654	2.0	641.1	1.7	276.6	2.8	546.6	2.4	50.8	2.6	25 644.4	226	2 030.6	48.9	85.3
United Kingdom	70	2.0	7 562	2.7	1 502.6	4.1	508.5	5.2	1 033.0	4.6	48.5	2.5	21 466.0	108	692.3	67.2	68.7
United States	102	3.0	37 020	13.1	6 171.7	16.8	1 834.4	18.9	3 872.6	17.3	458.9	23.3	60 507.0	363	4 499.4	49.6	62.7
Federal Republic of Germany	32	0.9	6 299	2.2	322.9	0.9	122.3	1.3	274.2	1.2	58.1	3.0	10 091.2	197	1 816.8	19.4	84.9
Other European countries	51	1.5	14 449	5.1	9 012.7	24.5	1 599.3	16.5	7 157.2	32.0	256.7	13.1	176 720.2	283	5 033.8	110.7	79.4
Others	205	6.0	23 483	8.3	1 345.8	2.6	427.8	4.4	780.8	3.5	92.0	4.7	6 564.9	115	448.8	18.2	58.0

Note: Rubber processing and granite quarrying are excluded. The contribution of permanent residents under the Permanent Stay Scheme is included under "others".

Source: Singapore, Department of Statistics: *Report on the Census of Industrial Production, 1981* (Singapore, Namic Printers Pte Ltd., 1982), p. 5.

electronics, the second largest industry and largest employer in the manufacturing sector.

Japanese firms rank next in importance to Singapore, other European, and United States firms, accounting for 16 per cent of total manufacturing employment, 9 per cent of output and 10 per cent of exports, with a third-ranked average employment size of 243. Though they ranked sixth in terms of capital expenditure per establishment in 1981, and fifth in average output size, they had a low value-added per worker, below that of even Malaysian and Singapore firms.

Among firms of other nationalities, those from the Federal Republic of Germany stand out because of their greatest export orientation (85 per cent). But they rank low in terms of output and value-added per worker – a reflection of their concentration in the labour-intensive electronics and instrument manufacturing industries.

Among other Asian firms, those from Hong Kong are much larger than Singapore and Malaysian firms in average output and employment size (over 100 workers per establishment), and more heavily export-oriented.

The manufacturing sector in Singapore is clearly dualistic. It is dominated by large, highly export-oriented, more capital-intensive foreign enterprises, particularly from the United States and Western Europe, and in the petroleum and electronics industries. But there are also many small, more labour-intensive local enterprises that support these large firms. They complement rather than compete with the large foreign-owned enterprises. Whereas the foreign firms (with the exception of the Malaysians) are largely export-oriented, the local firms produce mainly for the domestic market. Their output includes not only consumer goods but also intermediate inputs and subcontracted items for foreign-owned firms.

The capital market is highly developed and venture capital is readily obtainable at reasonable interest rates. The multinational companies which dominate the manufacturing sector bring their own capital with them, or borrow on the local market. Because Singapore is a financial centre and the headquarters of the Asian dollar market, it receives a net capital inflow from outside the country which serves to depress domestic interest rates, and provides a source of funding for investments in other countries of the region. Most enterprises are private, limited liability companies, and few companies, especially foreign companies, are listed on the local stock exchange. New rights and share issues are always oversubscribed, indicating a surplus of risk capital available for investment. Thus foreign and local capital and entrepreneurship are in abundant supply in Singapore.

Capital from abroad and domestic savings play a crucial role in accelerating the growth of the Singapore economy. In 1982 total capital formation amounted to 49 per cent of GDP, probably the highest rate in the world. Gross national savings, which included retained profits of firms and individual savings in the Central Provident Fund (CPF), and banks and other financial institutions provided about two-thirds of the national savings and compulsory CPF savings. Funds from foreign sources accounted for only a third of the financing of capital formation.

Workers and labour markets

From 1957 to 1982 annual labour force growth has averaged 3.7 per cent a year (table 34). This rapid rate of labour force growth since 1957 reflects not only the rate of population growth with a lag of about 15 years but also the increasing labour force participation rate of women and the employment of foreign labour.

Female labour

Female labour force participation increased most during the boom years of the late 1960s and early 1970s, when export manufacturing operations employing large numbers of women were being established. It slowed down during the 1974-75 recession when females accounted for most of the lay-offs in the manufacturing sector, and climbed again during the late 1970s. The rate of female labour force participation has risen from less than 20 per cent in 1966 to 45 per cent in 1982. It increases with educational level (see table 35), and declines with age from a peak of 79.4 per cent for women aged 20-24 years. It is also higher for single than for married women.[4]

Women have increased their proportion of the labour force from 18 per cent in 1957 to 26 per cent in 1970 and 35.7 per cent in 1982. Between 1970 and 1982 they more than doubled their number in the labour force, while the male labour force increased by only 36 per cent. Working women are over-represented relative to men in lower value-added industries and occupations, and under-represented in higher value-added ones. They earn on average 64 per cent of male incomes and are concentrated in relatively few, female-intensive occupations and industries. They account for nearly half of all workers in the manufacturing sector. The most common occupation for a woman in Singapore is that of electrical or electronic equipment or component assembler.

Increased female labour force participation and increased employment of foreign labour together accounted for 55 per cent of total labour force growth between 1970 and 1980; in 1980 women and non-citizens together made up 42 per cent of the Singapore labour force. The increase in female labour force par-

Table 34. Labour force and its rate of growth, 1957-82

	1957	1970	1980	1982	Average annual growth rate (%)		
					1957-70	1970-82	1957-82
Persons	471 918	726 676	1 115 958	1 170 485	3.4	4.1	3.7
Male	387 708	539 223	730 606	752 598	2.6	2.8	2.7
Female	84 210	187 453	385 352	417 887	6.3	6.9	6.6

Sources: Singapore Department of Statistics: *Report on the Census of Population, 1957* (Singapore, Government Printers, 1964) p. 84; idem: *Census of Population, 1980*, release No. 4 (Singapore Singapore National Printers 1981), p. 6; Singapore, Ministry of Labour: *Report on the Labour Force Survey of Singapore, 1982* (Singapore, Photoplates Private Ltd. 1983), p. 29.

Table 35. *Labour force participation rate by sex and education, 1966-82*

Level of education	1966			1970			1975			1980			1982		
	Persons	Male	Female	Persons	Male	Female	Persons	Male	Female	Persons	Male	Female	Persons	Male	Female
Total	42.3	64.4	19.8	45.6	67.3	23.6	48.4	66.9	29.6	55.9	72.0	39.3	63.4	81.5	45.2
No qualifications	46.5	85.1	19.7	34.7	78.3	15.0	35.9	59.6	17.7	35.0	55.9	19.9	47.0	76.7	26.9
Primary	32.4	46.7	11.5	44.9	63.6	19.3	48.5	63.7	28.9	62.2	75.7	44.9	63.8	80.7	42.6
Secondary	76.8	90.7	50.9	54.2	65.7	38.6	74.3	81.4	65.9	76.8	81.5	71.9	77.1	84.4	69.4
Upper secondary	91.5	96.7	82.4	59.9	64.8	53.1	78.4	87.3	63.6	83.4	89.7	74.3	77.4	84.9	67.6
Tertiary	–	–	–	69.6	76.9	49.8	85.8	93.7	65.0	89.7	97.0	74.9	89.7	96.6	77.0
Qualification n.e.c.	–	–	–	–	–	–	44.9	76.3	5.0	–	–	–	68.2	81.7	49.3

Sources: Singapore, Ministry of National Development and Economic Research Centre: *Singapore Sample Household Survey, 1966* (Singapore, Government Printing Office, 1967), p. 116; Singapore, Ministry of Labour and National Statistical Commission: *Report on the Labour Force Survey of Singapore, 1975* (Singapore, International Press, 1976), pp. 26, 38; Singapore, Department of Statistics: *Report on the Census of Population, 1970*, Vol. I (Singapore, Government Printing Office, 1973), p. 125; idem: *Census of Population, 1980*, release No. 4 (Singapore, Singapore National Printers, 1981), p. 5; Singapore, Ministry of Labour: *Report on the Labour Force Survey of Singapore, 1982* (Singapore, Photoplates Private Ltd, 1983), pp. 22, 31.

ticipation is the result of both demand and supply factors in the labour market. On the demand side, rapid economic growth and industrialisation, especially the establishment of export manufacturing industries like electronics and garments, expanded employment opportunities for women. On the supply side, smaller family size, more education for women, changes in social attitudes, the need for greater family income in a rising-cost urban environment, and the location of labour-intensive export factories in densely populated public housing estates all encouraged and facilitated the entry of more women into the labour force.

Foreign labour

The employment of foreign labour in Singapore is regulated by government immigration policy, which is designed to meet domestic labour imbalances, to increase the skills and improve the quality (in genetic, educational and occupational terms) of the local population, and to instil in it desirable social values and work habits (hard work, thrift, etc.) possessed by foreign workers.[5]

As early as 1968 temporary foreign workers were allowed into the country to satisfy the labour requirements of export manufacturing industries. By 1973 foreign workers reportedly numbered over 100,000, or one-eighth of the total Singapore labour force. Most of them were from Peninsular Malaysia. During the 1974-75 recession lay-offs, especially in the export manufacturing industries, reduced the number of foreign workers, which did not increase again until 1978, particularly in the booming manufacturing and construction sectors. By 1980 there were 120,000 non-citizen workers. Since then it has continued to increase, especially in the labour-short booming construction sector. In addition to workers from Peninsular Malaysia, increasing recruitments were made of workers from "non-traditional" sources, including Indonesia, Thailand, Sri Lanka, India and Bangladesh.

Foreigners working in Singapore include both unskilled "guest workers" on temporary employment permits, and skilled workers, professionals and entrepreneurs who are encouraged to obtain permanent residence and settle in Singapore, especially if they are ethnic Chinese from other Asian countries. Unlike in some European countries, unskilled foreign workers in Singapore do not acquire a right to bring their families to Singapore regardless of the number of years they have spent on the island. However, skilled workers who have acquired permanent residence status are allowed to bring their families. Foreign workers are over-represented at the highest and lowest ends of the skill spectrum, as measured by educational, occupational or income levels (table 36). At the low end they are concentrated in production jobs in the construction and manufacturing sectors – in the latter, mostly females in the export-oriented textile, garment, leather, wood and wood product industries. At the high end they are over-represented in administrative and managerial occupations, and are mostly male. At the same educational and occupational level foreigners receive higher mean incomes than Singapore citizens, with the exception of foreign female employees in the lowest educational and occupational groups, who earn less than their citizen counterparts.

Table 36.   Summary statistics on the characteristics of resident and non-resident workers in Singapore, 1980

	Singapore residents		Non-residents
	Citizens	Non-citizens	
1. Number	957 607	40 208	79 275
(a) % female	34.9	28.2	31.1
(b) % Chinese	79.4	49.7	56.1
(c) % Malays	13.5	25.5	18.4
(d) % aged 30	53.2	32.7	60.1
(e) % single	47.5	29.0	55.9
2. % no qualification/primary	72.1	77.7	74.7
3. % tertiary	2.8	8.3	10.7
4. % in manufacturing	28.6	34.0	46.1
5. % in construction	5.5	8.4	20.2
6. % in trade	22.3	22.1	9.4
7. % in personal and household services	3.3	7.0	7.4
8. % of manufacturing workers in:			
(a) textile, garments and leather	12.9	19.9	27.8
(b) wood and wood products	5.8	10.2	12.8
(c) electrical and electronics	27.2	23.2	16.6
(d) transport equipment	11.3	10.8	11.1
9. % professional and technical	8.7	9.6	9.9
10. % administrative and managerial	4.4	7.3	8.6
11. % clerical and sales	30.0	19.1	5.3
12. % production and related workers	38.2	45.5	64.5

Source: Compiled from tables in Singapore, Department of Statistics: *Census of Population, 1980*, release No. 4 (Singapore, Singapore National Printers, 1981).

The increased employment of foreigners is largely the result of a greater demand for labour than could be supplied by the citizen labour force, especially in unskilled labour-intensive industries like construction and shipbuilding (for males), electronics, textiles and woodworking (for females), and in highly skilled professional, technical, administrative and managerial occupations. The supply of foreign workers is controlled by government immigrant policy, which has tended to follow market forces, that is, tightening supply during recessions, and liberalising it during booms. The government policy is to phase out by 1991 all unskilled foreign labour, and encourage the permanent immigration of skilled foreigners. Labour from "non-traditional" country sources is to be gradually phased out by 1986 (except for construction, shipyards and domestic service), and Malaysian labour by 1991. In January 1984 the Government announced that Hong Kong, the Republic of Korea and Macau will be considered as traditional sources of foreign labour, and employers can recruit skilled workers from these sources on two-year renewable permits until 1991.[6]

Employment structure and productivity growth

While the availability of foreign labour contributed to output growth by increasing labour supply, it has also slowed labour productivity growth. Productivity grew by 5 per cent annually in the first half of the 1960s and accelerated to 7 per cent during 1966-74 as a result of rapid capital formation. Labour productivity growth slowed to less than 4 per cent a year from 1975-77 and to less than 3 per cent by the end of the 1970s, partly because of the Government's wage restraint policy that emphasised job creation rather than efficient use of labour. In consequence, labour inputs accounted for 71 per cent of total output growth in the 1970s.[7]

As shown in table 37, productivity growth has been slower in the sectors which have been expanding most rapidly in terms of output and employment (manufacturing and financial and business services). In the late 1970s productivity actually declined in construction, and rose very slowly in manufacturing, the two sectors employing the largest number and proportion of foreign workers. This slowdown in productivity growth and the unwanted increasing dependence on foreign unskilled labour were two of the major factors that led to the economic restructuring and wage correction policies announced in 1979. Productivity growth accelerated to an annual rate of 5 per cent in 1980 and 1981 but fell to 2 per cent in 1982.[8] In 1983 it rose again to 4 per cent reflecting mainly improved economic performance. Higher productivity gains since 1980 have,

Table 37. Rate of growth of real GDP per worker, 1966-82

Industrial sector	1966-73	1974-76	1977-82
Total	7.0	2.9	3.9
Agriculture and fishing	2.5	12.3	12.1
Quarrying and mining	17.0	17.5	1.5
Manufacturing	9.7	4.5	1.6
Utilities	7.0	3.8	17.2
Construction	6.1	14.1	0.5
Commerce	5.4	−5.2	2.8
Transport, storage and communications	7.6	9.3	8.7
Finance, insurance, real estate and business services	11.0	−3.1	5.4
Other services		4.8	4.4

Sources: Singapore, Ministry of National Development and Economic Research Centre: *Singapore Sample Household Survey, 1966* (Singapore, Government Printing Office, 1967), pp. 132-137; Singapore, Department of Statistics: *Singapore National Accounts, 1960/73* (Singapore, Singapore National Printers, 1975), p. 29; idem: *Yearbook of Statistics, 1982/83* (Singapore, Singapore National Printers, 1983), pp. 56, 78.

however, not reduced the need for foreign workers, especially in the construction sector. Since 1981 the Government has relaxed rules on the importation and retention of foreign workers several times. The announcement in January 1984 that employers can import workers from such newly defined "traditional" sources as Hong Kong, Macau and the Republic of Korea suggest that official short-run policy on foreign labour remains flexible and responsive to employer feedback.

As employment expanded, its structure changed. As table 38 shows, since 1957 the proportion of the total workforce employed in the primary and tertiary sectors of the economy has declined, while that in the secondary sector has increased. The number of people employed in agriculture, forestry and fishing, mining and quarrying has fallen in absolute terms. The most dramatic growth in numbers has occurred in manufacturing employment, which increased by almost five times between 1957 and 1982, to become the largest employer in the economy, accounting for 30 per cent of total employment. Trade is the second largest employer in the economy, followed by other services, and transport and communications. Although finance, insurance and business services rank fifth in employment, they registered the second fastest rate of employment growth after manufacturing, increasing more than four times between 1957 and 1982.

Table 38. Working persons by industrial sector, 1957-82

Industrial sector	1957		1970		1980		1982	
	No.	%	No.	%	No.	%	No.	%
Total	471 918	100.0	650 892	100.0	1 077 090	100.0	1 140 507	100.0
Agriculture, forestry and fishing	32 668	6.9	22 458	3.5	16 962	1.6	11 528	1.0
Mining and quarrying	1 601	0.3	2 168	0.3	1 139	0.1	2 578	0.2
Manufacturing	67 365	14.3	143 100	22.0	324 121	30.1	335 970	29.5
Utilities	4 038	0.9	7 615	1.2	8 464	0.8	7 855	0.7
Construction	24 628	5.2	43 126	6.6	72 346	6.7	71 850	6.3
Trade	131 353	27.8	152 910	23.5	229 759	21.3	253 545	22.2
Transport and communications	50 347	10.7	79 041	12.1	119 917	11.1	129 817	11.4
Finance, insurance and business services	20 383	4.3	23 071	3.5	79 412	7.4	89 812	7.9
Public administration, community, social and personal services	137 439	29.1	177 022	27.2	224 554	20.9	235 522	20.7
Activities not adequately defined	2 096	0.4	381	0.1			2 030	0.2

Sources: Singapore, Department of Statistics: *Report on the Census of Population, 1970*, Vol. I (Singapore, Government Printing Office, 1973), p. 179; idem: *Census of Population, 1980*, release No. 4 (Singapore, Singapore National Printers, 1981), p. 13; Singapore, Ministry of Labour: *Report on the Labour Force Survey of Singapore, 1982* (Singapore, Photoplates Private Ltd., 1983), p. 41.

Table 39. *Working persons by two-digit manufacturing industries, 1957-82*

Industry	1957		1970[1]		1975		1980[1]		1982[2]	
	No.	%	No.	%	No.	%	No.	%	No.	%
Total manufacturing	76 837	100.0	143 100	100.0	218 096	100.0	324 121	100.0	271 531	100.0
31 Manufacture of food, beverages and tobacco	9 204	12.0	14 391	10.1	14 125	6.5	16 543	5.1	13 312	4.9
32 Textile, wearing apparel and leather industry	14 023	18.3	25 939	18.1	38 803	17.8	48 193	14.9	37 602	13.8
33 Manufacture of wood and wood products	12 056	15.7	14 740	10.3	17 480	8.0	21 868	6.7	13 737	5.1
34 Manufacture of paper and paper products, printing and publishing	6 323	8.2	11 264	7.9	12 014	5.5	18 790	5.8	17 108	6.3
35 Manufacture of chemicals and chemical products, petroleum, coal, rubber and plastic products	9 518	12.4	15 601	10.9	23 758	10.9	24 840	7.7	20 712	7.6
36 Manufacture of non-metallic mineral products except petroleum and coal products	3 577	4.7	4 941	3.4	4 167	1.9	5 187	1.6	5 181	1.9
37 Basic manufacturing industries	2 759	3.6	2 942	2.1	3 464	1.6	2 850	0.9	2 228	0.8
38 Manufacture of fabricated metal products, machinery and equipment	13 850	18.0	46 194	32.3	99 631	45.7	178 404	55.0	155 044	57.1
39 Other manufacturing industries	5 527	7.2	7 088	4.9	4 654	2.1	7 446	2.3	6 607	2.4

[1] Working persons aged 10 years and over.   [2] Preliminary and establishments engaging 10 or more workers.

Sources: Singapore, Department of Statistics: *Report on the Census of Population, 1957* (Singapore, Government Printers, 1964), p. 84; idem: *Report on the Census of Population, 1970*, Vol. II (Singapore, Government Printing Office, 1973), pp. 94-95; Singapore, Ministry of Labour and National Statistical Commission: *Report on the Labour Force Survey of Singapore, 1975* (Singapore, International Press, 1976), p. 51; Singapore, Department of Statistics: *Census of Population, 1980*, release No. 4 (Singapore, Singapore National Printers, 1981), pp. 84-87; idem: *Yearbook of Statistics, 1982/83* (Singapore, Singapore National Printers, 1983), pp. 101-102.

The pattern of manufacturing employment has become much more concentrated by industry since 1957. The proportion of manufacturing workers
employed in every two-digit industry declined between 1957 and 1982, with the
exception of the manufacture of fabricated metal products, machinery and equipment, which increased its employment by 13 times to account for 57 per cent of
all manufacturing workers in 1982 (see table 39). This industry includes the
major labour-intensive export industries of electronics, electrical and instrument
assembly and shipbuilding. Together with the other major labour-intensive
export industries, textiles, wearing apparel and leather, they increased their share
of total manufacturing employment from 36 per cent in 1957 to 71 per cent in
1982.

The electrical and electronics industry employed some 110,000 persons
or 39 per cent of all manufacturing workers in 1981. Transport equipment and oil
rigs (mainly shipbuilding and repairing) employed 28,000 workers, or 10 per cent
of total manufacturing employment, while textiles and garments employed
35,000, or 13 per cent of the total. These three labour-intensive export industries
thus account for 62 per cent of all manufacturing workers in 1981. No other
industry accounted for more than 5 per cent of total manufacturing employment.

Structural change has altered not only the industrial pattern of employment but also occupational patterns. As table 40 shows, the proportion of high-
level, i.e. professional, technical, administrative and managerial workers has
risen with economic diversification while that for lower-level sales, clerical, and
service workers has fallen. However, the proportion of production and related
workers has remained at around 39 per cent.

Table 40. *Working persons by occupation, 1957-82*

Occupation	1957		1970		1980		1982	
	No.	%	No.	%	No.	%	No.	%
Total	471 918	100.0	650 892	100.0	1 077 090	100.0	1 140 507	100.0
Professional and technical	22 689	4.8	56 080	8.6	95 145	8.8	106 253	9.3
Administrative and managerial	8 891	1.9	15 476	2.4	52 175	4.8	58 272	5.1
Clerical	56 209	11.9	82 941	12.7	167 473	15.6	186 911	16.4
Sales	85 758	18.2	102 628	15.8	131 977	12.3	153 158	13.4
Services	73 615	15.6	88 744	13.6	112 196	10.4	124 235	10.9
Agricultural workers and fishermen	36 909	7.8	26 943	4.1	20 954	1.9	15 385	1.3
Production and related workers	187 163	39.7	254 949	39.2	434 996	40.4	439 076	38.5
Not classifiable	684	0.1	23 131	3.6	62 174	5.8	57 216	5.0

Sources: Singapore, Department of Statistics: *Report on the Census of Population, 1957* (Singapore, Government Printers, 1964), p. 85; idem:
Census of Population, 1980, release No. 4 (Singapore, Singapore National Printers, 1981), p. 15; Singapore, Ministry of Labour: *Report on the
Labour Force Survey of Singapore, 1982* (Singapore, Photoplates Private Ltd., 1983), p. 44.

Table 41. *Average hourly earnings by industry (all workers), 1972-82 (S$)*

Industrial sector	1972	1973	1974	1975	1976	1977	1978	1979	1980	1981	1982	Average annual percentage change 1972-82
All industries	1.64	1.81	2.15	2.45	2.56	2.73	2.86	3.12	3.52	4.04	4.67	11.0
Agriculture and fishing	1.26	1.74	2.21	2.43	2.15	2.36	2.42	2.70	3.19	3.61	4.42	13.4
Mining and quarrying	1.39	1.95	2.29	3.38	3.36	3.68	4.10	4.64	5.33	7.08	7.63	18.6
Manufacturing	1.29	1.41	1.66	1.94	2.01	2.14	2.26	2.48	2.79	3.25	3.62	10.9
Electricity, gas and water	1.63	1.86	2.28	2.47	2.67	2.90	3.16	3.45	3.90	4.04	5.31	12.5
Construction	1.56	1.65	1.93	2.12	2.28	2.53	2.71	2.95	3.33	4.03	4.07	10.1
Commerce	1.51	1.68	1.97	2.23	2.43	2.58	2.77	3.05	3.57	4.21	4.65	11.9
Transport, storage and communications	1.84	2.06	2.39	2.66	2.81	2.97	3.09	3.48	3.85	4.22	4.97	10.4
Finance, insurance, real estate and business services	2.51	2.64	3.23	3.40	3.60	3.90	4.08	4.43	4.96	5.44	6.24	9.5
Community, social and personal services	2.06	2.33	2.91	3.08	3.20	3.36	3.62	3.90	4.38	4.97	6.37	12.0

Sources: Singapore, Ministry of Labour: *1976 Singapore Yearbook of Labour Statistics* (Singapore, Photoplates Private Ltd., 1977), p. 41; idem: *1982 Singapore Yearbook of Labour Statistics* (Singapore, Photoplates Private Ltd, 1983), p. 41.

Table 42. *Average hourly earnings by type of worker, 1972-82 (S$)*

Type of worker	1972	1973	1974	1975	1976	1977	1978	1979	1980	1981	1982	Average annual percentage change 1972-82
Total	1.64	1.81	2.15	2.45	2.56	2.73	2.86	3.12	3.52	4.04	4.67	11.0
Professional, administrative, managerial and related workers	4.69	5.23	6.08	6.72	7.10	7.47	7.81	8.27	9.14	10.40	12.10	9.9
Clerical, sales, service and related workers	1.43	1.58	1.85	2.09	2.15	2.27	2.45	2.64	2.96	3.26	3.69	9.9
Production, transport and other manual workers	1.04	1.16	1.36	1.54	1.63	1.70	1.81	2.00	2.27	2.64	2.94	11.0

Sources: Singapore, Ministry of Labour: *1976 Singapore Yearbook of Labour Statistics* (Singapore, Photoplates Private Ltd., 1977), pp. 41, 43, 45, 47; idem: *1982 Singapore Yearbook of Labour Statistics* (Singapore, Photoplates Private Ltd., 1983), pp. 41-44.

Table 43. *Percentage distribution of employees by income and occupation and distribution of mean income by sex, 1982*

Monthly income (S$)	Total	Professional and technical workers	Administrators and managers	Clerical workers	Sales workers	Service workers	Agricultural workers and fishermen	Production and related workers	Workers not classifiable by occupation
Total	100.0	100.0	100.0	100.0	100.0	100.0	100.0	100.0	100.0
Below 200	6.1	0.7	0.1	0.7	4.1	10.4	7.4	2.8	60.4
200-399	28.6	5.4	0.4	24.6	26.0	44.1	40.5	37.2	18.9
400-599	27.2	11.4	3.0	37.4	25.8	26.0	28.2	33.3	7.9
600-799	14.1	13.4	6.5	18.7	15.2	8.5	12.3	15.9	4.3
800-999	6.7	11.1	8.2	8.9	7.9	4.7	4.7	5.5	2.0
1,000-1,499	8.6	25.5	25.7	7.5	11.5	4.3	4.7	3.9	3.2
1,500-1,999	3.0	13.1	12.4	1.5	3.2	1.0	1.0	0.8	1.3
2,000-2,499	2.1	7.6	13.2	0.4	2.8	0.5	0.3	0.4	0.9
2,500-2,999	0.8	2.9	5.7	0.1	0.8	0.2	0.2	0.1	0.2
3,000 and over	2.7	8.8	24.7	0.2	2.7	0.4	0.7	0.2	1.0
Mean income in dollars:									
Persons	739	1 464	2 239	614	795	483	521	525	368
Male	840	1 687	2 346	691	904	583	556	593	363
Female	549	1 123	1 677	570	491	378	369	345	636

Source: Singapore, Ministry of Labour: *Report on the Labour Force Survey of Singapore, 1982* (Singapore, Photoplates Private Ltd., 1983), pp. 53-55.

The labour market has functioned well in terms of allocating labour among economic sectors and occupations in response to changing supply and demand. Labour has shifted from the primary and tertiary sectors of the economy towards manufacturing, and from sales, service and agricultural occupations towards professional and technical, managerial and administrative, and clerical occupations in the course of economic diversification.

Earnings

Table 41 shows that average hourly earnings for the economy rose two-and-a-half times to S$4.67 (US$2.30) between 1972 and 1982, an increase of 11 per cent a year. Of the key sectors, financial and business services pay the most, while manufacturing pays the least. Except for the very small mining and quarrying sector, the variation in average increase in hourly earnings among sectors since 1972 is fairly small.

Production, transport and other manual workers, the lowest-paid workers, enjoyed the most rapid increase in earnings of 11 per cent a year between 1972 and 1982, 4 percentage points faster than the consumer price index. The best-paid group of workers – professional, administrative, managerial and related workers who earned almost five times more than production workers in 1982 – experienced earnings growth of 9.9 per cent, just 1 percentage point behind that of production workers. In consequence, the earnings gap between high-level workers and production workers has narrowed slightly (table 42).

Female workers earned on average 65.4 per cent of male income. The gap between male and female incomes is smallest among administrators and managers (71.5 per cent of male incomes) and widest among production and related workers (58.2 per cent). Mean monthly income for all employees in 1982 was S$739 (table 43). The highest mean incomes in 1980 are earned in financial and business services, and the lowest in agriculture and fishing, closely followed by manufacturing (table 44). The lowest paid workers are female manufacturing workers, who receive about 54 per cent of the mean income of all workers, and only 45 per cent of the mean income of male manufacturing workers. Their concentration in labour-intensive export manufacturing industries accounts for their low mean incomes.

Labour mobility and workers' attitudes

Workers in Singapore have always been highly responsive to market incentives, as suggested by the fact that they are mostly immigrants and the descendants of recent immigrants who left their homelands in search of better economic opportunities. Labour mobility is particularly high among young and lowly paid manufacturing and service workers, so much so that many employers consider "job hopping" a serious problem, especially during boom times.

Because Singapore is a city State, most workers were used to urban wage employment even before the advent of large-scale industrialisation. Thus prob-

Table 44. Average monthly income of employees by industry and sex, 1980 (S$)

Industrial sector	Persons	Male	Female
Total	585	677	430
Agriculture and fishing	512	552	331
Quarrying	804	813	758
Manufacturing	523	708	317
Utilities	644	649	609
Construction	504	511	437
Trade	555	655	401
Transport and communications	656	690	517
Financial and business services	929	1 188	606
Other services	561	556	571

Source: Singapore, Department of Statistics: *Census of Population, 1980*, release No. 7 (Singapore, Singapore National Printers, 1981), p. 7.

lems associated with adjusting to factory work and discipline have not been serious. For women workers, especially those from rural origins, there were some initial difficulties in the early years, for example in electronics assembly line operations requiring rotating shift work, but these difficulties have diminished with work experience and industrial upgrading.

In the early stages of development income was clearly the priority of workers, and probably remains so today. Most workers have little choice over hours worked, which are standardised at 44 hours per week for the public sector, and either 40 or 44 hours a week in the formal private sector. Labour force data indicate that average weekly hours worked since 1974 have been slightly less than 44 hours, suggesting little overtime work by employees. Since 1974 there has been a slight drop in median working hours, which together with widespread reports of increasing reluctance of workers to perform shift and overtime work, indicate a growing preference among workers for leisure. In a growing number of factories the norm is a five- rather than the more usual five-and-a-half-day week.

The labour movement and development

The evolution of the labour movement in Singapore was briefly discussed in Chapter 1. This section expands on the earlier discussion. Since self-government in 1959 the union movement has come increasingly under the dominance of the ruling party and government bureaucrats. Government bureaucrats have been involved in the running of the umbrella National Trades Union Congress (to which more than 90 per cent of all registered unions are affiliated) through its Labour Research Unit. Until the late 1960s NTUC leaders were mostly men with trade union experience. In the late 1970s the ruling party began appointing scholars and bureaucrats without union experience to key positions in the NTUC as part of its effort to make the labour movement more responsive to national priorities. In 1978 a non-unionist Member of Parliament (MP), Lim

Chee Onn, was put in charge of the NTUC as its Secretary-General; in 1980 he was made a Cabinet Minister without Portfolio. In 1983 Lim was removed from his position in the Cabinet by the Prime Minister because his leadership style had apparently antagonised "grass-roots" union leaders. His removal suggests that "grass-roots" union leaders are still influential, even though their power has diminished greatly. Ong Teng Cheong, then the Minister of Communications, replaced him. Like Lim, he too had no previous union experience but he is known to have a low-key style.

In the late 1970s a group of non-union MPs were appointed as "advisers" to individual unions, and in 1981 it was announced that advisory councils of MPs, government officials and other ruling party members would be formed to exert tighter control over unions at a time when government policy is to break up the large industrial unions like the Singapore Industrial Labour Organisation and the Pioneer Industries Employees' Union first into industry-based unions, and then into individual house or company unions.

Table 45 shows the growth and distribution of employees' trade unions and union membership by industry from 1970 to 1982. During this period the number of unions declined by 13 per cent while union membership nearly doubled. Union membership peaked at nearly a quarter of a million in 1979 but has fallen steadily since then and accounted for 19 per cent of employed persons in 1982. The utilities sector is most highly unionised, with union members accounting for 53 per cent of all workers in 1970 and 77 per cent in 1982. In transport and communications, union members represent 34 per cent of all workers in 1982, up from 15 per cent in 1970. Union membership as a proportion of all workers in financial and business services has fallen during the period from 22 per cent to 11 per cent. Nearly a fifth of all manufacturing workers were union members in 1982, an increase of 11 per cent since 1970.

The increase in union membership since the late 1960s did not lead to increased industrial action, thanks to the various legal, administrative and political moves which progressively pacified the unions. The number of man-days lost through work stoppages fell from a high of 410,891 in 1961 to a low of 2,514 in 1970, while the number of work stoppages declined from a high of 116 in 1961 to none in 1969 (table 46). This record of labour peace has continued into the 1970s, with only one stoppage in 1977, and none at all since then.

Current plans to reorganise the labour movement stem less from the need to curb strikes (which are legally permissible only under restrictive circumstances) than to mobilise workers for increased productivity. There is great official interest in adapting aspects of the Japanese industrial relations system (which is actually much more strike-prone than that in Singapore). The encouragement of company or house unions where workers can identify their interests more closely with those of employers is an example. The Government believes that increased company loyalty among workers will increase productivity and reduce political pressures for the Government to provide social and welfare benefits. There has been some worker resistance, for example from the United Workers of Petroleum Industry, to house unions, and the NTUC itself fears that such unions may not have enough good leaders.

Table 45. *Employees' trade unions by industry, 1970-82*

Industrial sector	1970		1973		1976		1980		1982	
	Number of trade unions	Member- ship	Number of trade unions	Member- ship	Number of trade unions	Member- ship	Number of trade unions	Member- ship	Number of trade unions	Member- ship
Total	102	112 488	92	191 481	91	221 936	83	243 841	89	214 337
Agriculture and fishing	2	231	2	372	2	393	1	374	1	279
Mining and quarrying	1	481	1	292	1	251	–	–	–	–
Manufacturing	22	10 218	21	31 111	17	33 999	16	34 325	22	59 007
Electricity, gas and water	6	4 044	10	11 061	10	15 628	3	6 460	3	6 087
Construction	3	1 723	3	1 619	2	1 395	2	1 469	2	1 321
Commerce	10	7 799	11	12 547	10	16 102	10	17 070	9	15 987
Transport, storage and communications	19	12 015	16	20 059	18	24 254	16	31 624	16	43 822
Finance, insurance, real estate and personal services	6	5 003	6	5 803	5	7 600	5	8 342	4	9 499
Community, social and personal services	29	43 478	19	43 460	24	49 656	28	60 150	29	60 188
Activities not adequately defined	4	27 496	3	65 157	2	72 658	2	84 027	3	18 147

Sources: Singapore, Ministry of Labour: *1976 Singapore Yearbook of Labour Statistics* (Singapore, Photoplates Private Ltd., 1977), pp. 106-107; idem: *1982 Singapore Yearbook of Labour Statistics* (Singapore, Photoplates Private Ltd., 1983), pp. 94-95.

Table 46.   Industrial stoppages and man-days lost, 1960-82

Year	Number of industrial stoppages	Number of man-days lost
1960	45	152 006
1961	116	410 891
1962	88	164 936
1963	47	388 219
1964	39	35 908
1965	30	45 800
1966	14	44 762
1967	10	41 322
1968	4	11 447
1969	–	8 512 [1]
1970	5	2 514
1971	2	5 449
1972	10	18 233
1973	5	2 295
1974	10	5 380
1975	7	4 853
1976	4	3 193
1977	1	1 011
1978	–	–
1979	–	–
1980	–	–
1981	–	–
1982	–	–

[1] Refers to man-days lost on account of a work stoppage which began in 1968.

Sources: Singapore, Department of Statistics: *Yearbook of Statistics, 1967* (Singapore, Government Printing Office, 1968), p. 24; idem: *Yearbook of Statistics, 1970* (Singapore, Government Printing Office, 1971), p. 30; Singapore, Ministry of Labour: *1976 Singapore Yearbook of Labour Statistics* (Singapore, Photoplates Private Ltd., 1977), pp. 109-110; idem: *1982 Singapore Yearbook of Labour Statistics* (Singapore, Photoplates Private Ltd., 1983), pp. 96, 98.

Labour unions in Singapore have contributed to the development process by helping to ensure the labour peace necessary to attract private investment, especially foreign investment, and by ensuring a stable, productive workforce. Union representatives also sit with government and employers' representatives on tripartite policy-making bodies like the National Wages Council, Economic Development Board, and Jurong Town Corporation. In unionised companies collective bargaining and other negotiations between unions and employers pay close attention to national policy guide-lines developed by the tripartite boards. The current attempt to decentralise unions and union-management negotiation to the level of the individual firm may return some power to the unions. But the raising of labour productivity will require active participation by unions or other workers' representatives.

The role of government

As discussed in Chapter 1 above, the Government of Singapore plays a heavily interventionist role in the country's economic development. The following sections outline the various policies, their objectives and results, focusing especially on policies affecting export manufacturing.

Investment incentives

The Government through the Economic Development Board (EDB) plays the leading role in promoting desired investments, particularly of manufacturing industries. To promote investments in desired industries the Government has expanded and modified its tax incentives to reflect its changing priorities (see Chapter 1).

Despite rising wages and labour shortages, Singapore's attractiveness as an investment location has grown rather than diminished over the years. The labour-intensive industries that were set up in Singapore in the late 1960s and early 1970s have adjusted by upgrading their operations rather than by relocating their entire operations. For these industries as well as those set up in the last few years a predictable, stable environment is probably more important than tax incentives alone.

Trade policies

Historically, Singapore grew because of its free-port status. Since independence the Government has continued the colonial policy of free trade. Over the years, with economic success, official belief in free trade and competition has strengthened. The Government has removed most of the protective tariffs established during the early 1960s and has introduced policies to deter price-fixing among domestic producers and importers. By spurring competition among importers, it can help to minimise imported inflation. Government commitment to competition is unlikely to waver in the future.

Monetary policy

Given the extreme openness of the Singapore economy, the scope for domestic monetary policy is limited.[9] Since the late 1960s the role of monetary policy has been accommodative; its main objectives were to counter the deflationary impact of government surpluses and the withdrawal of spending power out of the income stream through compulsory contributions to the Central Provident fund, and to prevent severe fluctuations in domestic interest rates and to maintain a strong, stable Singapore dollar.

In the early 1970s, when the secondary market was undeveloped, the Monetary Authority of Singapore, the country's quasi-central bank, varied minimum cash balances and bank deposit and lending rates to achieve economic stability. But these measures were ineffective against import-induced inflation. After 1975 when banks were free to set interest rates, the Authority resorted more to open market operations and variations of rediscount rates to influence money supply and domestic interest rates. But the inactive market for government securities constrained the effectiveness of these instruments. Since the complete liberalisation of foreign exchange controls in June 1978 the Authority's ability to control money supply by varying statutory minimum reserve requirements has weakened further and the burden of monetary management has fallen largely on exchange rate policy.

Basically the Authority now manages monetary policy by influencing the exchange rate of the Singapore dollar against a trade-weighted basket of foreign currencies. It does not, unlike the Hong Kong Government, try to influence interest rates directly. However, by influencing the exchange rate through intervention in the foreign exchange market, the Authority influences the inflow of foreign capital which in turn affects domestic interest rates.

Monetary and exchange rate policies in Singapore are delicately balanced to achieve several different, and often conflicting objectives: to maintain Singapore's attractiveness as a financial centre (which requires exchange rate stability); to minimise imported inflation (helped by exchange rate appreciation); and to preserve the international competitiveness of Singapore's manufactured exports (harmed by exchange rate appreciation).

Fiscal policy

Like monetary policy, fiscal policy in Singapore has generally not been employed in a counter-cyclical fashion to influence macro-economic variables.[10] It also does not have a clear redistributive objective or impact. Its objectives partly reflect social goals of discouraging luxury consumption and promoting thrift and awareness of the cost of government services by widening the income tax net. But its main objective is to stimulate the growth and restructuring of the economy.

The income tax net now covers two-fifths of the working population compared with less than one-tenth at independence. This has occurred naturally through economic growth and rising incomes. But vigorous attempts have also been made to include the self-employed, including hawkers and taxi drivers, in the tax net. When first voted into power, the ruling People's Action Party, in line with its socialist ideology of the time, raised the top marginal rate of the progressive rate structure from 50 to 55 per cent. During the following 20 years there were no major changes in personal income tax rates or deductions. In the late 1970s a policy of reducing tax rates was introduced as a work incentive. It has benefited mostly middle- and high-income earners.

Table 47 shows the sources of government revenue for selected years from 1960 to 1982. Government revenue multiplied 30 times between 1960 and 1982, and nearly seven-and-a-half times between 1970 and 1982. As a result of rapid growth and inflation the share of receipts from personal and corporate income as a proportion of total government revenue has risen from 20 per cent in 1970 to 36 per cent in 1982. In 1982 direct tax revenues accounted for less than a third of total government revenue, down 13 percentage points since 1970. In-

Table 47. **Percentage distribution of economic classification of government revenue, 1960-82 [1]**

Government revenue by item	1960	1970	1980	1981	1982 [2]
Total (US$ thousand million)	0.3	1.2	5.5	7.1	9.0
	(100%)	(100%)	(100%)	(100%)	(100%)
Transfer receipts	72.1	70.3	75.1	73.7	69.2
Taxes on income	24.4	20.6	34.5	36.9	36.1
Taxes on production and expenditure	45.1	42.7	37.1	33.1	30.0
Excise duties	3.2	8.6	4.4	3.7	3.1
Import duties	29.9	14.8	7.8	6.0	5.3
Property tax	1.8	8.9	9.7	9.0	9.0
Motor vehicle taxes [3]	2.1	4.9	8.9	7.3	6.8
Stamp duties	1.2	1.9	2.9	3.9	2.8
Others	6.9	3.6	3.4	3.2	3.0
Other transfer receipts	2.6	7.0	3.5	3.6	3.2
Estate duty	1.3	0.8	0.5	0.7	0.5
Others	1.3	6.2	3.0	2.9	2.8
Sales of goods and services	17.2	20.5	15.2	19.6	22.6
Interest and dividends received	5.3	8.7	7.9	6.6	8.0
Other receipts	5.4	0.5	1.8	0.1	0.1

[1] Government revenue refers to receipts credited to Consolidated Revenue Account. [2] Preliminary. [3] Motor vehicle taxes comprise road tax, special tax on heavy oil engines, *ad valorem* registration fees and passenger vehicle seating fees. It does not include import duties on imported motor vehicles.

Source: Singapore, Ministry of Trade and Industry: *Economic Survey of Singapore, 1982* (Singapore, Singapore National Printers, 1983), p. 126.

direct taxes are levied mainly on luxury items such as motor vehicles, liquor, tobacco and petroleum products. There is no general sales tax.

Property tax receipts accounted for 9 per cent of total government revenue. There is no capital gains tax. Taxes on trade, that is import duties, which accounted for nearly a third of government revenue in 1960 contributed only 5.3 per cent in 1982, largely because of the progressive reduction and elimination of tariffs.

Total tax revenues provide more than two-thirds of all government revenue in 1982, the remainder being accounted for by sales of goods and services (23 per cent) and interest and dividends received (8 per cent). In 1982 tax and non-tax government revenue together accounted for 28 per cent of GDP, and more than covered government current expenditure.

Table 48 shows current government expenditure by functional category for selected years from 1960 to 1982. Spending on defence, justice and police accounted for nearly a fifth of government expenditure in 1982. Spending on health, education and other social and community services took up another 17 per cent, while servicing of public debt (largely domestic debt owed to the Central Provident Fund which provides the Government with a ready source of development finance) accounted for a third of total government spending. Over the years, spending on defence has increased much faster than spending on health and education services.

Table 48. Percentage distribution of functional classification of government current expenditure, 1960-82 [1]

Expenditure item	1960	1970	1980	1981	1982 [2]
Total (US$ thousand million)	0.2	1.0	5.2	5.8	8.4
	(100%)	(100%)	(100%)	(100%)	(100%)
General services	9.5	5.6	4.1	3.1	3.3
Defence, justice and police	14.1	31.2	25.6	23.3	19.2
Social and community services	45.4	29.5	19.9	19.8	17.1
Education	23.6	16.9	10.9	10.9	10.3
Health	13.4	8.0	4.3	4.4	3.7
Others	8.4	4.6	4.7	4.5	3.1
Economic services	10.7	6.7	4.4	5.0	4.6
Public debt	4.1	20.9	34.7	46.2	34.7
Transfer to development fund	8.2	3.7	9.9	1.6	20.2
Unallocatable	8.0	2.5	1.4	1.0	0.9

[1] Government current expenditure refers to payments from Consolidated Revenue Account.   [2] Preliminary.

Source: Singapore, Ministry of Trade and Industry: *Economic Survey of Singapore, 1982* (Singapore, Singapore National Printers, 1983), p. 128.

Government development spending amounted to about a third of government current expenditure. Like current government spending, government capital spending expanded greatly in the 1960s and 1970s. In recent years government capital spending included spending on the development of the new Changi International Airport, roads and bridges, land reclamation and development, schools and junior colleges. In the 1980s construction of a mass rapid transit system estimated to cost S$5,000 million will claim a good portion of government expenditure. Besides direct development expenditure, the Government has also provided loans to statutory boards and industrial and commercial enterprises. Most of the loans to statutory boards were for public housing and industrial estate development.

Labour market policies

Before the formation of the National Wages Council in 1972, wage determination was decentralised. After 1972 wage changes were influenced greatly by the Council's annual guide-lines which were designed to promote orderly wage changes. The Council's guide-lines have helped to contain wage increases in a tight labour market and so to maintain Singapore's competitive edge in international markets. But they have also deterred, until the wage corrective policy of 1979-81, economic upgrading and efficient use of increasingly scarce domestic labour.

The Council's success in minimising industrial conflicts and ensuring orderly wage changes has ironically also produced conditions that might undermine its influence in the future. By strongly guiding wage developments the Council has inhibited the growth of close ties between workers and employers at the company level. Workers increasingly think that the NWC, whose policies reflect government priorities, is the body that gives them wage increases. The Government's primary role in the NWC also made employers dependent on the Council to assure industrial peace. In consequence, they did not pay enough attention to ways to gain worker loyalty.

Equally important, the NWC eroded flexibility in wage negotiations. Both unions and employers became essentially implementers of NWC decisions. Differences in productivity and profitability among employers were not fully reflected in wage changes, resulting in labour misallocation.

The Government recognises that a bigger role for market forces in wage developments is necessary to strengthen worker-employer relations and to improve labour market efficiency. It also recognises that the NWC still has a role to play in helping the economy to make the transition from a guided wage system to a freer labour market.

In 1980 the NWC, to promote productivity, introduced a "second-tier" wage increase linked to an individual's productivity. But employers and employees were not happy with the implementation of the "second-tier" increase because it demoralised those not receiving it rather than spurring productivity. The Council stopped recommending specific second-tier increases the following year. Since then it has encouraged wage flexibility in wage negotiations by recommending a range of wage increases.

Besides guiding wage increases through the Council, the Government's hand is highly visible in other labour market areas. It influences the supply of labour through its population control and immigration policies. Government policy on labour importation has two objectives – to alleviate short-run labour shortages and to upgrade skills and quality of the population by granting permanent residence and citizenship to skilled workers who can be assimilated without difficulty into the local population (see the section on workers and labour markets above).

The Government is also planning changes to the 1968 labour laws in line with its aim of strengthening ties between workers and employers. The "confrontational" assumptions of present labour legislation relating to collective bargaining will be removed. There will be a more restrictive definition of union prerogatives, and the relationship between employers and employees will be redefined to encourage worker-employer co-operation.

Education and manpower training

Expenditure on education formed the largest part of the Government's budget in the early years of its rule. Investment was concentrated first on expanding the primary, and then secondary, school systems, through the building of new schools and the training of teachers. In the late 1960s there was increasing emphasis on technical education. Opportunities for technical, vocational and professional training increased gradually in the 1970s. In the last few years with the launching of the "Second Industrial Revolution", they have been expanded greatly (see Chapter 1).

In the 1960s and 1970s the educational system was characterised by high wastage and frequent policy changes. In 1980 the Government began reforming the education system to reduce wastage and to bring it more in line with social and economic conditions of Singapore in the 1980s. The reforms essentially created different streams of education for primary and secondary students according to their abilities.[11]

Beyond basic literacy, the acquisition of industrial and other skills necessary for a modern economy took place informally throughout the 1960s and most of the 1970s. That is, human capital was developed by work experience rather than by formal training. This was possible because of the relatively low levels of technology and skill required in most manufacturing industry. In recent years, with the emphasis on skill and technology upgrading, formal manpower training in industrial skills has become a high priority of government policy. Formal post-secondary technical institutions in Singapore include the National University of Singapore (whose engineering school is to be oriented to the training of research and design engineers), the Nanyang Technological Institute (a new institute to train production engineers for manufacturing industry), the Singapore Polytechnic, Ngee Ann Technical College, and the Vocational and Industrial Training Board, all of which train various levels of technicians and skilled workers, and award formal diplomas. These institutes must greatly enlarge their enrolment to meet the Government's manufacturing growth and upgrading targets. They may find difficulty in getting enough qualified Singaporeans. Indeed, some institutions, e.g. the National University of Singapore, have had to take in a growing number of Malaysians into departments that cannot meet the enrolment targets set by the Council of Professional and Technical Education, a high-level body that directs the production of skilled and professional manpower. In return for full tuition and scholarship grants, Malaysians are required to work for a specific period in Singapore or for Singapore firms abroad. In this way, the Singapore Government ensures that its investment in the education of foreigners benefits the country.

In August 1983 the Prime Minister voiced concern about the lower marriage and reproduction rate of women graduates which he suggested may lead in the long term to a lower-quality population and a talent shortage. Since then, steps have been taken by various institutions, including the National University of Singapore, to increase opportunities for interaction between young men and women.

Social legislation and welfare policies

The socialist philosophy of the newly elected PAP Government in 1959 favoured progressive social legislation and welfare policies. For the next 20 years the Government expanded the provision of public social services – notably health, sanitation, education, housing and recreational facilities, available to the population free, or at nominal, low, and subsidised cost. The objective was not only to ensure that the basic needs of the mass of the population were quickly met – which secured for the Government a large measure of its political support – but also to contribute to economic growth and industrial development. Improved health and education represented an investment in human capital which would pay off in more productive workers, while mass public housing at low cost represented an implicit subsidy to low real wages in manufacturing. The provision of subsidised public social services therefore contributed to the competitiveness of labour-intensive export manufacturing – by "buying" the support of the working classes, thus ensuring political stability and labour peace, and by ensuring that low wages did not imperil basic standards of living.

Social legislation and policies also played a part in ensuring an adequate supply of low-wage labour for the labour-intensive export industries. As early as 1960 the Government enacted a Women's Charter which improved the legal position of women and granted them equal rights with men in many areas. Educational opportunities for women were expanded. A comprehensive family planning programme was vigorously implemented, and rapidly succeeded in reducing family size from a six- to a two-to-three-child norm. "Protective" labour legislation prohibiting night work by women was removed, and maternity leave and benefits instituted in employment provisions. Light industrial estates were located in the new public housing estates so that workers could be employed near their homes. All these policies contributed to a dramatic increase in female labour force participation in the 1960s and 1970s. With a stronger legal position, fewer children, the ability to work night shifts in factories and easy access to factory jobs, women entered the job market in increasing numbers in the 1970s.

But by the late 1970s the positive effects of earlier social policies were, from the Government's point of view, tapering off. The Government now feels that rising affluence and the high income elasticity of demand for social services like health, housing and public transportation are causing excess demand for these facilities, the costs of which have been rising over time. It also feels that workers have become too dependent on the State to provide their basic needs, a dependence that affects their productivity and reduces their loyalty to employers. Government policy now is to reduce state subsidies on most social services for most of the population, and encourage companies to provide more benefits to their workers in return for increased loyalty and productivity. Government efforts to reduce subsidies on public services have already begun in middle-income public housing and in public transportation, and is being extended to health and medical services. In 1984 it was intended that the Government would introduce a Medisave scheme to which workers must contribute and from which they can withdraw funds to pay for their medical expenses.

Company welfare schemes for employees have their limitations. Most obviously, it is practicable only in large firms, and will increase their labour and overhead costs. What may be gained in workers' loyalty may be lost in greater rigidity of the workforce. As the Singapore population ages, those schemes which bind workers to their companies may limit quick responses to changing conditions. (The Japanese are already facing the problem of what to do with immobile workers past their prime.) They also imply that the wage system must be set on a life-cycle basis, rather than being linked to year-to-year productivity changes. In the Japanese system this means that young workers are underpaid and older workers overpaid, relative to their individual productivity. Singapore workers, on the other hand, expect to climb upward rapidly in their jobs and so would be unhappy with a system that does not reward quickly for good performance.

In the export manufacturing sector company welfare schemes have other limitations besides raising labour and overhead costs. The multinational corporations which dominate this sector may not be willing to develop the long-term obligations and commitments to workers in one location that such schemes imply. The economics of international relocation of industry dictate that such firms must have the freedom to relocate production as costs and market conditions change. Many export industries are also highly cyclical – such as petroleum and electronics in Singapore – and do not favour strong worker-company attachments as these reduce the flexibility and speed of their adjustment to new conditions. The new high-technology industries that Singapore is encouraging are all capital-intensive, embody rapidly changing technology, and face rapidly changing markets.

Political factors

Political stability, and popular support for all the above government policies, have been achieved by two factors. One is the ruling Government's success in "delivering the goods" to the population in terms of providing promised jobs, schools, housing, and other social services. The other is its excellent grassroots political machinery. On coming to power in 1959 the PAP very quickly developed a wide and comprehensive network of grass-roots community organisations – the People's Association (PA) which runs community centres and kindergartens in each neighbourhood, citizens' consultative committees in each electoral constituency, even PAP kindergartens for young children, and so on. By providing physical and social facilities and grass-roots leadership, these organisations played an important role in mobilising support for the Government's survivalist ideology and the policies which it justified.

At the formal political level, Members of Parliament serve their constituencies as channels for individuals' requests, complaints, and petitions to the all-powerful bureaucracy. They serve more as intermediaries between the public and the state machinery than as makers of policy (which is decided at the highest levels of political office and of the bureaucracy).

Since 1979 many changes in the PAP's leadership and grass-roots organisation have been introduced to "meet the times". At the political level, "older generation" Members of Parliament and even Cabinet Ministers (those in their forties and fifties) have been retired to "make way for new blood" in the ruling party's quest for "self-renewal". Unlike the older MPs, the "second echelon" leaders, both ministers and MPs, do not start off with a grass-roots political base. Most are technocrats and professionals recruited for political office from the bureaucracy itself, and from the private sector. They are selected for office by the top political leaders, rather than chosen by the people "from the bottom up". While the rise of technocrats has been meteoric in some cases, their fall can be just as fast, as the removal of Lim Chee Onn from his general secretaryship of the NTUC suggests. Lim's experience has apparently dampened the enthusiasm of technocrats for political careers, and the PAP is reportedly finding it difficult to recruit willing and able candidates for political office.

There has also been a simultaneous proliferation of grass-roots organisations. Residents' Committees have been formed, especially in public housing estates where nearly 80 per cent of the population live, to bring younger and more highly educated participants into community leadership and management. This has led to some competition and duplication among the various community organisations.

The PAP may in fact have over-reached itself in trying to manage the grass-roots. An overbearing and arrogant style of leadership, and elitism in the appointment of young "leaders" who are perceived as having little in common with "the common people", are beginning to cause some resentment. This is seen as one of the reasons behind the PAP's first electoral defeat in 18 years, in a November 1981 by-election which put a sole opposition candidate in Parliament as the representative of a solidly working-class district.

Another proximate cause of this defeat is the people's dissatisfaction with the Government's promise that it will no longer be delivering the "goods" which they have come to expect, and will not intervene to improve the lot of the poor who are disproportionately affected by the rising cost of necessities like housing and transportation. This reflects the PAP's tough-minded philosophy of eschewing "soft options" or subsidies for basic needs, and of developing greater "self-reliance" among working people. It sees increased productivity as the means towards higher incomes from which people can then afford to pay for more expensive goods and services. This, however, takes time, and does not alleviate immediate hardships.

For over 20 years the PAP has maintained itself in absolute power with the consent of the electorate in Singapore. The population's apparent political apathy results both from depoliticisation and from the complacency born of rising affluence. Its electoral setback in 1981, which even Prime Minister Lee Kuan Yew conceded was not a bad thing, has caused the ruling party to change its style, though not its basic policies. The party is paying much greater attention than before 1981 to public reactions to its policies.

Recognising that its grass-roots organisations may have reached the limits of their effectiveness, the Government is in fact trying to make the civil service itself more attuned to and involved with the grass-roots – for example, by developing community relations departments in the police and armed forces, and involving young government officials in grass-roots organisations.

Summary on the role of the State

The role of the State in Singapore can be differentiated according to two different stages of economic development. From 1959 to 1979 the Government played an active interventionist role in the economy. Many of its policies – investment incentives, infrastructural development, exchange rate policy, labour, wage, and immigration policy, and so on – were geared to ensuring the competitiveness of labour-intensive export manufacturing industries. Wages were kept low, and workers' basic needs subsidised by government social services, which won for the ruling party widespread political support.

Since 1979 the Government has launched three new "experiments" which are expected to change the economic, social, and political face of Singapore. The economic experiment involves restructuring and upgrading into higher-value activities, particularly in the manufacturing sector. There was for three years a corrective wage policy to spur labour productivity. The social experiment involves transforming the Singaporean social personality into one which is more collectivist rather than individualist in its orientation, and more self-reliant rather than State-reliant for the provision of basic needs.[12] The State's social responsibilities are to be increasingly transferred to private employers, in order to develop a strong link between productivity and social benefits. The political experiment involves the appointment of "second generation" political leaders who are technocrats and professionals rather than grass-roots politicians, and whose task is to carry out the economic and social experiments.

In broad terms, these experiments reflect the Government's philosophical and ideological shift across the political spectrum from "left" to "right". Its early democratic socialist principles and policies which laid the social and political foundations for a spectacularly successful State-guided but market-oriented economic development programme are being de-emphasised in favour of greater private initiative and social responsibility at the company level. There are social, political, and economic costs as well as benefits to such a shift, and its outcome – particularly in terms of popular acceptance of the new policies – remains to be seen.

Appraisal

The above sections have suggested the relative roles of the three main actors – enterprises, workers and the Government – in the development process in Singapore. The Government is clearly the leader in this process – in terms of formulating priorities, developing and carrying out policies, and influencing or even directing the decisions and actions of the other two groups.

That there has been little conflict between the Government and private sector enterprises results from the fact that the Government's programmes and policies are essentially guided by market forces. It recognises the primacy of the private sector in deciding what, how much, how and for whom to produce, and does not interfere in production and marketing decisions. At most, it seeks to influence these decisions in desired directions by means of various investments and subsidies. Government policies are usually, though not always, in the interests of business, especially big and foreign business.

There is also little conflict between business and labour, largely because of the Government's intermediary role in their relationship. Workers' rights and powers have been curbed by government legislation, and the Government itself controls the union movement. It has promoted unionisation as a means of extending its control over the labour force in the private sector. In the 1970s annual wage increases were decided by the tripartite National Wages Council, thus removing a potential source of conflict between employers and workers.

The peaceful co-operation of workers with employers and with the Government has been achieved by political, economic, and social means. Politically, there is the ruling party's origins in and close identification with the labour movement, and its subsequent control of the national union leadership. Economically, workers have clearly benefited from the Government's development policies and from their employers' prosperity. It is thus easy to persuade them that their economic interests are identical with those of firms and of the nation as a whole. Socially, workers have also benefited from government social subsidies which have compensated for low wages by raising real standards of living. The Government has therefore managed to explain to workers the rationale for its various pro-business policies, and to secure their acceptance of these policies as being in the national, and hence in workers' own interests.

The relationship among workers, employers and the State will change in the years to come, given the Government's new policy to reduce workers' dependence on the State, and to decentralise employer-worker relations to the company level. The Government will, however, maintain strong control over even company unions, though it hopes that such unions will be even more closely identified with individual company interests than the present industry-wide unions. "Privatisation" of many state functions may increase productivity and ensure a lean, competitive economy, as indicated. But it may also increase income disparities.

In the more liberalised economy of the 1980s there may be a stronger role for private enterprise, but the Government is likely to maintain its leadership in the determination of national economic policy. Firms may have greater freedom to operate at the firm level, but within an institutional and incentive framework established by the Government. Workers' dependence on the State may lessen and their dependence on employers increase, but this relationship will also be defined and approved by the State.

Notes

[1] Singapore, Department of Statistics: *Census of Population, 1980*, release No. 4 (Singapore, Singapore National Printers, 1981).

[2] See, for example, Linda Y. C. Lim: "Chinese business, multinationals and the state: Manufacturing for export in Malaysia and Singapore", in Linda Y. C. Lim and L. A. Peter Gosling (eds.): *The Chinese in Southeast Asia: Ethnicity and economic activity*, Vol. I (Singapore, Maruzen Asia, 1983), pp. 245-274.

[3] The employment figures for 1975 are low because of the impact of the 1974-75 recession.

[4] For details on female labour force participation, see Linda Y. C. Lim: *Women in the Singapore economy*, Occasional Paper Series No. 5 (Singapore, National University of Singapore, Economic Research Centre, 1981).

[5] *Straits Times* (Singapore), 14 January 1984.

[6] For a detailed discussion of foreign labour in Singapore, see Pang Eng Fong and Linda Y. C. Lim: "Foreign labor and economic development in Singapore", in *International Migration Review*, Fall 1982, Vol. 16, No. 3, pp. 548-576.

[7] See Pang Eng Fong: "Economic development and the labour market in a newly industrializing country: The experience of Singapore", in *The Developing Economies*, Mar. 1981, Vol. XIX, No. 1, pp. 3-16.

[8] Singapore, Ministry of Trade and Industry: *Economic Survey of Singapore, 1982* (Singapore, Singapore National Printers, 1983).

[9] For an analysis of the conduct and limits of monetary policy in Singapore, see John R. Hewson: "Monetary policy and the Asian dollar market", in Monetary Authority of Singapore: *Papers on Monetary Economics* (Singapore, Singapore University Press for the Monetary Authority of Singapore, 1982), pp. 171-194.

[10] For an analysis of Singapore's tax system, see Mukul Asher and Susan Osborne (eds.): *Issues in public finance in Singapore* (Singapore, Singapore University Press, 1980).

[11] For a discussion of Singapore's educational system, see Seah Chee Meow and Linda Seah: "Education reform and national integration", in Peter Chen (ed.): *Singapore: Development policy and trends* (Singapore, Oxford University Press, 1983), pp. 240-267.

[12] See Linda Y. C. Lim and Pang Eng Fong: "The making of a new Singaporean", in *Sunday Times* (Singapore), 26 July 1981; and Pang Eng Fong and Linda Y. C. Lim: "Labouring towards a new stereotype", in *Sunday Times* (Singapore) 9 August 1981.

Chapter 4

Industry studies: electronics and textile and garments

Electronics

Electronics has been a "priority" industry of the Singapore Government since the late 1960s. It is a complex and diversified international industry whose dynamic technological and market characteristics reflect the changes in the Singapore manufacturing sector.[1]

In the 1960s technological and market changes in electronics led to world-wide sourcing and the multinationalisation of the industry. Electronics manufacturers developed an international division of labour, in which labour-intensive products and processes were located in low-wage developing countries, while R & D, and more skill- and capital-intensive production were retained in the developed countries which were the home markets of the parent companies. The developing countries of East and South-East Asia became the favoured off-shore manufacturing locations of electronics MNEs from North America, Western Europe, Australia and Japan. Over time, this international division of labour within the vertically integrated MNE and between the different host and home countries has changed to reflect changing comparative advantages. Increasingly complex and skill- and capital-intensive stages of production, including some R & D activities, are being moved offshore to newly industrialising economies like those of Hong Kong, the Republic of Korea and Singapore, while the simpler and more labour-intensive stages are being moved to countries like Indonesia, the Philippines, India, Sri Lanka and Bangladesh where labour is cheaper.

In 1965 the electronics industry in Singapore consisted of one local firm assembling television sets and radio kits for the small, protected domestic market. In 1968, attracted by the plentiful, low-cost, disciplined labour then available, and by generous tax incentives offered to labour-intensive export manufacturers, semi-conductor multinationals based in the United States began establishing offshore plants in Singapore. This marked the start of a period of phenomenally rapid growth up to early 1974, with Japanese and European consumer and component electronics multinationals following the American lead. Most major electronics multinationals in the world established a subsidiary in Singapore to produce for the world market – from the United States came Texas Instruments, National Semiconductor, Hewlett Packard, Fairchild and General Electric; from Japan, Hitachi, Toshiba, Matsushita and Sanyo; from Europe, Philips, Siemens, Thomson and SGS/Ates.

By 1974 the electronics industry in Singapore employed over 46,000 workers, or over one-fifth of the total manufacturing workforce, and accounted

Table 49. Aggregate data on the electronics industry in Singapore, 1970-81 [1]

Year	Number of establishments	Number of workers	% of manufacturing workforce	Output (S$m)	% of manufacturing output	Output per worker (S$'000)	Value-added per worker (S$'000)	Average remuneration per employee (S$'000)	Direct export as % of total sales	Direct export as % of total manufacturing direct export
1970	35	11 251	9.3	212.8	5.5	18.9	8.8	2.1	73.9	9.3
1971	49	15 874	11.3	319.0	6.8	20.1	8.9	2.7	84.8	14.4
1972	53	27 270	16.0	616.8	10.8	22.6	10.5	2.9	93.0	16.0
1973	64	39 210	19.7	1 096.8	13.8	28.0	10.8	3.3	92.8	19.7
1974	91	46 247	22.4	1 603.6	12.0	34.7	14.5	3.9	92.4	18.8
1975	95	32 026	16.7	1 457.9	11.6	45.5	14.8	5.2	90.9	18.1
1976	105	43 718	21.1	1 987.8	13.0	45.5	14.6	5.0	91.0	19.2
1977	115	46 441	21.2	2 322.7	13.3	50.0	15.2	5.4	90.6	19.0
1978	135	53 440	21.9	2 821.9	14.3	52.8	16.7	5.6	89.5	19.8
1979	168	66 844	24.8	4 092.7	15.5	61.2	19.1	6.3	86.5	21.0
1980	172	71 727	25.1	5 344.0	16.3	74.5	23.3	7.1	87.1	23.5
1981	185	69 358	24.6	5 728.5	15.6	82.6	23.4	8.3	86.4	22.3

[1] For 1970-79, industry covers codes 38211/12, 38321, 38322, 38329. For 1980-81, code has been changed to 384.

Source: Singapore, Department of Statistics: *Report on the Census of Industrial Production, 1970-81*.

for S$1,600 million or 12 per cent of total manufacturing output (table 49). Then the severe world recession of 1974-75 caused a fall in output and a drop in employment of 14,000 workers, or nearly one-third of total industry employment by the end of 1975. Recovery began in 1976, and by 1981 industry output had grown to S$5,500 million (US$2,700 million), or 16 per cent of total manufacturing output and 22 per cent of manufactured exports (both second only to petroleum refining). Electronics remains the largest employer in the manufacturing sector, with 69,358 workers, or 25 per cent of the total manufacturing workforce, in 1981. Between 1970 and 1981 output in the industry grew at the average rate of 35 per cent a year, while employment rose at 18 per cent a year. Since 1976 S$1,300 million of new capital has been invested in the industry, which remains heavily export-oriented. There are 200 large and small, domestic and foreign electronics manufacturing firms in Singapore, with at least another several hundred in supporting industries.[2] Multinationals from the United States, Japan and Europe dominate all sectors of the industry in terms of output, exports, capital investment and employment.

Since 1981 the industry has undergone another dramatic change with the arrival of firms manufacturing computer components and peripherals. These fast-expanding firms include most of the leading names in the field including Tandon, Seagate, Apple, NEC, and Digital Equipment Corporation. Their phenomenal growth in the last two years has helped greatly to boost the expansion of the electronics industry. In less than three years since 1980, Singapore has emerged as the largest exporter of disk drives in the world.[3]

Table 50 presents disaggregated data on the electronics industry. The largest sector in both employment and output is component manufacturing – the manufacture of semi-conductors and other electronic components, and communications equipment and apparatus (Industrial Code 38322 until 1974 and 38329 since 1979). Employment in this sector nearly quadrupled between 1970 and 1974, fell sharply between 1974 and 1975, and since 1975 has been rising, though at a much slower rate than in the early 1970s. The second largest sector comprises firms manufacturing radio and television sets, sound reproducing and recording equipment (Industrial Code 38321). Employment changes in this consumer electronics sector are less dramatic than in the component manufacturing sector, with less labour being shed in the 1974-75 recession. Since then, employment in this sector has risen more rapidly than that in the component sector, now amounting to half that in the component sector compared with one-third in 1974. Both sectors export between 85 and 90 per cent of their output. The other two sectors – manufacture of gramophone records (Industrial Code 38322 since 1975) and data processing equipment and office machinery (Industrial Code 38211/12) – are fairly small.

Between 1968 and 1980 the electronics industry created over 60,000 new jobs or one-third of manufacturing employment growth. Most of these jobs have been for unskilled or semi-skilled female production operators who account for 80 per cent of total employment in the industry, compared with 51 per cent for the manufacturing sector as a whole in 1980. The female intensity of employment in this industry has remained fairly constant over time, while average remuner-

Table 50. Principal statistics of sectors of the electronics industry in Singapore, 1970-81

Item	1970	1971	1972	1973	1974	1975	1976	1977	1978	1979	1980	1981
Code 38211/12												
Manufacture and repair of data processing equipment and office machinery, except photocopying machines												
Number of establishments	–	–	–	–	10	12	12	9	12	12	6	5
Number of workers	–	–	–	–	3897	3427	4150	3594	4887	5507	3124	3308
Value added (S$m)	–	–	–	–	120.2	86.1	79.5	114.1	96.5	140.4	132.3	160.2
Value added per worker (S$'000)	–	–	–	–	30.8	25.1	19.2	31.8	19.7	25.5	42.3	48.4
Total sales (S$m)	–	–	–	–	220.0	180.0	186.3	213.2	207.5	289.9	288.3	364.1
Direct export as per cent of total sales (%)	–	–	–	–	95.8	96.0	94.7	96.9	94.2	95.4	94.1	87.3
Capital spending/employee remuneration	–	–	–	–	0.67	0.70	0.57	0.50	0.48	0.24	0.52	0.41
Code 38321												
Manufacture of radio and television sets, sound reproducing and recording equipment												
Number of establishments	7	9	11	14	19	22	20	21	23	39	46	45
Number of workers	2917	3851	7245	9565	11226	9995	11486	13470	15165	22343	29786	27711
Value added (S$m)	12.2	25.9	56.1	65.3	88.7	104.2	108.4	155.7	170.7	301.5	523.0	548.8
Value added per worker (S$'000)	4.2	6.7	7.7	6.8	7.9	10.4	9.4	11.6	11.3	13.5	17.6	19.8
Total sales (S$m)	43.6	80.1	162.0	209.7	323.7	378.7	516.2	597.9	781.5	1332.7	1976.2	2129.3
Direct export as per cent of total sales (%)	53.0	76.6	88.4	89.5	91.5	89.2	90.0	88.4	89.2	86.4	87.5	88.5
Capital spending/employee remuneration	–	–	–	–	0.61	0.28	0.24	0.42	0.38	0.48	0.33	0.25
Code 38322 [1]												
Manufacture of gramophone records, radio, television and communication equipment and apparatus (including semi-conductors n.e.c.)												
Number of establishments	28	40	42	50	62	5	6	8	11	13	17	22
Number of workers	8334	12023	20025	29645	31124	261	298	550	1004	1131	1400	1541

Value added (S$m)	86.9	115.3	230.5	359.4	314.5	3.7	6.1	8.6	15.5	19.5	32.2	26.2
Value added per worker (S$'000)	10.4	9.6	11.5	12.1	10.1	14.3	20.5	15.6	15.4	17.2	23.0	17.0
Total sales (S$m)	165.2	235.9	441.9	904.8	042.6	11.5	14.4	22.3	42.0	52.5	69.2	83.6
Direct export as per cent of total sales (%)	94.8	93.6	94.5	93.5	91.9	46.4	50.0	45.1	20.1	35.5	31.7	29.7
Capital spending/employee remuneration	–	–	–	–	0.37	0.40	0.97	0.38	0.89	0.41	0.68	0.96

Code 38329
Semi-conductors and other electronic components and communications equipment and apparatus

Number of establishments	–	–	–	–	–	56	67	77	89	104	103	113
Number of workers	–	–	–	–	–	18 343	27 784	28 827	32 384	37 863	37 417	36 798
Value added (S$m)	–	–	–	–	–	280.9	443.6	426.6	610.6	812.1	981.3	890.5
Value added per worker (S$'000)	–	–	–	–	–	15.3	16.0	14.8	18.9	21.4	26.2	24.2
Total sales (S$m)	–	–	–	–	–	864.4	1304.9	1465.5	1769.5	2264.2	2841.7	3207.2
Direct export as per cent of total sales (%)	–	–	–	–	–	91.2	91.3	91.3	90.7	86.6	87.5	86.3
Capital spending/employee remuneration	–	–	–	–	–	0.37	0.36	0.41	0.50	0.72	0.61	0.68

Total

Number of establishments	35	49	53	64	91	95	105	115	135	168	172	185
Number of workers	11 251	15 874	27 270	39 210	46 247	32 026	43 718	46 441	53 440	66 844	71 727	69 358
Value added (S$m)	99.1	141.1	286.7	424.7	523.5	475.0	637.7	705.0	893.3	1273.6	1668.8	1625.7
Value added per worker (S$'000)	8.8	8.9	10.5	10.8	14.5	14.8	14.6	15.2	16.7	19.1	23.3	22.0
Total sales (S$m)	208.8	316.0	603.9	1114.6	1586.3	1434.6	2021.7	2298.9	2800.5	3939.3	5175.3	5784.1
Direct export as per cent of total sales (%)	73.9	84.8	93.0	92.8	92.4	90.9	91.0	90.6	89.5	86.5	87.1	86.4
Capital spending/employee remuneration	–	–	–	–	0.46	0.38	0.36	0.42	0.47	0.60	0.50	0.51
Electronics employment as percentage of manufacturing[2] employment (%)	9.3	11.3	16.0	19.7	17.5	16.7	21.1	21.2	21.9	24.8	25.1	24.6

[1] For the years 1970–74, code 38322 includes the manufacture of semi-conductors and other electronic components and communications equipment and apparatus. [2] Excluding rubber processing.
Source: Singapore, Department of Statistics: *Report on the Census of Industrial Production, 1970–81.*

ation in the industry has remained about 20 per cent below the average for the manufacturing sector as a whole.[4] Male and skilled workers comprise only a small proportion of workers in the industry.

Besides this direct employment creation, the electronics industry has also generated many new jobs indirectly through the purchase of inputs from both local and foreign-owned supporting industries. It buys 58 per cent of its inputs locally, 25 per cent from Japan, 9 per cent from Hong Kong, and the remaining 8 per cent from other sources including the United States.[5] According to one estimate, the number of indirect new manufacturing jobs created by the electronics industry in supporting firms which depend mainly on the industry is over 12,000.[6] If supporting firms in both the manufacturing and service sectors are included, indirect employment creation by the industry since 1968 exceeds 20,000 jobs.

Though it has directly and indirectly created probably over 80,000 new jobs and buys over half its material inputs locally, the Singapore electronics industry, dominated by multinational firms, has not developed many linkages with *locally owned* supporting firms. A significant proportion of locally bought inputs are purchased from foreign-owned subsidiaries in Singapore, set up by multinationals from the United States and Japan to supply parts to their subsidiaries and other customers in Singapore and neighbouring countries. Other inputs are purchased locally from traders, dealers and agents of foreign manufacturers who import them from abroad. Inputs produced in Singapore by locally owned supporting firms are often not competitive in price, range, quality and delivery with imported inputs or inputs manufactured by foreign subsidiaries: this is because of the smaller scale and shorter industrial experience of local firms. The market for domestic inputs is growing as the electronics industry becomes more integrated locally, and with financial support from the Economic Development Board and technical assistance from multinational customers, local supporting firms are likely to develop further.[7]

Now a major regional and world manufacturing centre for the international industry, the electronics industry in Singapore has undergone many changes in recent years. Labour-intensive operations still predominate, and productivity as measured by value-added per worker is still lower than the average for the manufacturing sector as a whole. But rapid growth and the very high rate of employment creation in this export-oriented industry have contributed to the tightening of the labour market and rising wages throughout the 1970s. Average remuneration per employee has risen five times since 1968, though it remains below the manufacturing average. Wage increases were particularly large in 1973 and 1974, and 1979-81, following National Wages Council guide-lines of double-digit percentage increases. Employment growth in the industry in the late 1970s has been slowed both by a serious shortage of female workers, necessitating the import of foreign workers, and by rising wage levels. The world and industry recession of 1981 occasioned some lay-offs, but growth since 1982 has been stronger than ever, especially in the booming new computer peripherals sector.

Labour productivity has been increasing at 4 per cent a year since 1975 (when labour productivity rose sharply because of the large fall in employment caused by the recession). Value-added per worker more than doubled in ten years. As table 50 shows, component manufacturing firms, which are generally more capital-intensive, generate higher value-added per worker than firms producing consumer electronics products. Over the years, the electronics industry in Singapore, led by the multinationals, has been upgrading its activities into higher-value, more skill- and capital-intensive, technologically complex products and processes. In the last few years, both local and foreign electronics manufacturers have begun transferring labour-intensive assembly activities out of Singapore, where their comparative advantage has been declining, to Malaysia and other neighbouring countries. Processes remaining in Singapore have been increasingly automated and mechanised, while newer, higher-value products have been introduced in response to both world product market competition and local labour market pressures. But there are limits to automation and mechanisation, especially in the computer manufacturing sector where rapid product changes place a great premium on flexibility which increases with labour flexibility.

A few of the larger multinationals have invested heavily in local product design and development engineering, but research and technology are still largely acquired from foreign parent companies. A major new development in the semi-conductor industry is the investment of the multinational – SGS/Ates – in local wafer fabrication, the very heavy, capital- and technology-intensive "front end" of semi-conductor manufacture.

Changes in the electronics industry have paralleled changes in the Singapore manufacturing sector. Wages and productivity in electronics, though they have risen considerably in absolute terms, have remained since 1975 at 81-85 per cent of the total manufacturing averages. The capital-labour ratio (as crudely measured by the ratio of capital to labour expenditures) rose from 0.38 to 0.51 in electronics between 1975 and 1981, and from 0.52 to 0.67 in all manufacturing. In 1981 the capital-labour ratio in the semi-conductor sector was 0.80, higher than the average for all manufacturing. Thus while electronics remains less capital-intensive than the manufacturing sector as a whole, the differential is narrowing quickly.

In the dominant multinational sector of the industry, production decisions, technology choice, employment creation and local linkages are determined primarily by international industry and product market factors, rather than by the management of the individual enterprises, local and labour market conditions, or host government policies.[8]

Although the multinationals originally located in Singapore to take advantage of available cheap labour for labour-intensive products, they have not so far been deterred from further investments by Singapore's rapidly rising wage costs, which are higher than those of other newly industrialising and developing countries. This is because wages in Singapore remain a fraction of wage costs in the multinationals' parent countries, and form only a small proportion – around 10 per cent for consumer electronics firms, and 1 per cent for computer manufacturing firms – of the total production costs of their local plants. Labour productivity has also risen more rapidly than wages. But the most labour- intensive products and sub-assemblies requiring simple skills have been moved out of Singapore to neighbouring countries, while the accumulated skills and experience of workers in the Singapore plants have encouraged the transfer to them of more technologically sophisticated, higher-value, capital- and skill-intensive products and processes. Automation has been introduced – in response to high labour turnover rates and the increasing reluctance of workers to perform routine, monotonous and accident-prone manual assembly tasks, in a tight labour market.

All these changes began for the most part *before* the Singapore Government introduced its wage correction policy in 1979. New capital investment benefits from government investment incentives, but it is not primarily motivated by these incentives, but rather by international product market and technological changes in the industry. However, Singapore's advantages – such as the excellent infrastructural services provided by public enterprises, institutional efficiency, social, political and financial stability – have contributed to its competitive advantage in attracting high-technology investments by multinational electronics firms.

The electronics industry in Singapore, except in the newer high-tech firms, is partly unionised, but workers have no say in production decisions, and wage determination is largely pre-empted by the setting of national wage guidelines by the Government as the leading partner in the NWC. In multinational subsidiaries management decisions are largely directed by the parent corporation's technological and market parameters. There is relatively little room for discretionary local decision-making, whether the local managers are expatriates (preferred by European and Japanese companies) or local citizens (preferred by companies in the United States). Thus, for example, local input sourcing is determined by cost, quality and availability, and has been increasing in all companies, regardless of nationality or individual corporate philosophy.

Local electronics companies, like the multinationals, are predominantly export-oriented, but are for the most part small enterprises concentrated in the labour-intensive, low-technology end of the industry, producing simple consumer goods and components, usually in some kind of subcontracting arrangement with foreign buyers of local multinational subsidiaries. Over the years, multinational electronics firms in Singapore have been developing supply linkages with local firms, providing them not only with orders, but with technological, and sometimes even financial and marketing assistance.[9] Simpler parts and sub-assemblies are subcontracted to local firms. The relationship between multinationals and local enterprises has evolved into an increasingly complementary rather than competitive one – partly because many of the local enterprises, including larger ones, which competed in product markets with the multinationals have since gone out of business or changed their product lines. Local and foreign firms remain competitive, however, in input markets.

Ever since the large influx of foreign firms and the expansion of manufacturing exports led by foreign firms in the late 1960s, local firms, while numerically larger than foreign firms, have declined in *relative* importance. In recent years the Government has provided various incentives to encourage small firms to upgrade their operations because it believes that a healthy local supporting industry is essential to the growth of the manufacturing sector. Since the intro-duction of the restructuring strategy there has been a surge in local investment commitments. In the mid-1970s local investment commitments amounted to less than 10 per cent. Since 1981 local share of total manufacturing investment com-mitments has risen sharply. In 1982 local investors committed S$540 million or nearly one-third of the total investment commitments of S$1,700 million in the manufacturing sector. As in the past, they will play for quite some time to come a supporting role in Singapore's climb up the technological ladder. The Singapore Government realises this and has not attempted to legislate a larger role for local enterprises in the Singapore economy. Unlike many governments, it is not overly concerned about the significant role of foreign capital in its development, believ-ing that strong foreign participation in its economy does not necessarily diminish a country's sovereignty.

Textiles and garments

The textile and garments industry, one of the earliest to be established in Singapore, has undergone many changes in the past 20 years. It began as a locally owned and operated industry, consisting of small-scale, cottage-like establish-ments producing mainly for the local market. The expectations of a Malaysian Common Market generated when Singapore joined the Federation of Malaysia in 1963 led to an influx of new investments, mainly by Chinese entrepreneurs from Hong Kong and elsewhere.

But the Malaysian Common Market failed to materialise, and Singapore left the Federation in 1965. With a newly established production capacity greater than could be sustained by the Singapore market alone, textile and garments manufacturers were forced to look to foreign markets. They began to sell, often under subcontracting arrangements with foreign buyers, to the developed countries. Because of Singapore's early entry into manufacturing for export to the West, it has a large country quota under the international Multi-Fibre Arrange-ment, which has sustained the industry since. For the first time in many years local export production is below the quota. This has attracted further investment by Chinese manufacturers from other countries and areas, such as Hong Kong, whose quotas are quickly exhausted. Singapore is thus used as a third country export manufacturing base.

The textile and garments industry in Singapore is labour-intensive and produces mainly cheap, consumer goods at the low value end of the market. In recent years the tightening domestic labour markets, rising wage and imported raw material costs, and an appreciating exchange rate, have undermined the com-petitiveness of the Singapore industry, compared with the increasing number of its competitors among the newly industrialising and developing countries. The industry has been protected by a continued small import tariff in the domestic market, and by the MFA quota in foreign markets. It remains one of the few lightly protected industries in Singapore despite Singapore's strong commitment to free trade and competition. One reason why Singapore has not scrapped

Table 51. Aggregate data on the textile and garments industry in Singapore, 1960-81

Year	Number of establishments	Number of workers	% of manufacturing workforce	Output (S$m)	% of manufacturing output	Output/workers (S$'000)	Value added per worker (S$'000)	Average remuneration per employee (S$'000)	Direct exports as % of total sales	Direct exports as % of total manufacturing direct exports
1960[1]	33	1 302	4.7	15.2	3.3	11.7	3.4	1.8	-	-
1965[2]	83	5 965	12.6	38.1	3.5	6.4	2.0	1.2	-	-
1970	211	17 038	14.1	170.4	4.4	10.0	2.8	1.7	57.5	6.3
1975	324	29 346	15.3	545.7	4.3	18.6	5.8	3.5	62.5	4.7
1980	473	36 898	12.9	1 337.2	4.2	36.2	11.5	6.0	63.5	4.4
1981	468	35 776	12.7	1 346.8	3.7	37.6	12.4	6.9	63.7	3.8

[1] Includes leather and footwear, except rubber footwear.   [2] Includes footwear, except rubber footwear.

Sources: Singapore, Department of Statistics: *Report on the Census of Industrial Production, 1960/61* (Singapore, Government Printing Office, 1964), p. 24; idem: *Report on the Census of Industrial Production, 1965* (Singapore, Government Printing Office, 1966), p. 19; idem: *Report on the Census of Industrial Production, 1970* (Singapore, Government Printing Office, 1972), p. 10; idem: *Report on the Census of Industrial Production, 1975* (Singapore, Photoplates Private Ltd., 1976), p. 17; idem: *Report on the Census of Industrial Production, 1980* (Singapore, Singapore National Printers, 1981), p. 67; idem: *Report on the Census of Industrial Production, 1981* (Singapore, Namic Printers Pte Ltd., 1982), p. 67.

import tariffs on textiles and garments is that the tariffs enable it to offer preferential rates to its ASEAN partners under the ASEAN preferential trading agreements. The industry has also kept labour costs low by relying heavily on imported foreign female labour, mostly from Malaysia and, more recently, also from Thailand. Foreigners comprise 27 per cent of all workers in the industry, and account for 30 per cent of all non-resident and 20 per cent of all non-citizen resident workers in the manufacturing sector as a whole.

Singapore's long-run declining comparative advantage in labour-intensive export manufacturing portends significant changes in the textile and garments industry. Textile firms, which contrary to popular belief are capital-intensive, are losing their competitive edge to other countries, including developed ones. The shortage of women operators has compounded their market difficulties. The more flexible and resilient garments sector has seen little new investment. A few firms in the sector have relocated. Those remaining are moving upmarket, producing higher-value items for department stores in developed countries. They have also automated some operations (e.g. pattern making, button-stitching) to increase productivity and save labour. Automation has been spurred by investment incentives such as the low-interest mechanisation grants given by the Skill Development Fund, and by the Trade Development Board's export quota allocation system which rewards upgrading firms. In the textile sector the Government hopes that long-run upgrading will lead to specialisation in the production of textile machinery rather than end-products for export.

Table 51 shows the growth of the textile and garments industry in Singapore over the past 21 years. There has been a steady increase in the number of establishments, workers, and total output except for a slight downturn in 1981. Since 1970 the industry has employed more than 14 per cent of all manufacturing workers, making it the second largest employer in this sector, next to electronics. However, it accounts for less than 5 per cent of manufacturing output and exports, although it exports 64 per cent of total sales. This indicates the very labour-intensive and low-value nature of textile and garments production. Output per worker, value-added per worker and average remuneration per employee have all risen steadily over the years, indicating increasing productivity and a trend of upgrading. But these figures remain well below the average for the manufacturing sector as a whole.

Table 52 disaggregates data on different sectors of the textile and garments industry. The largest sector is that producing shirts and other outer garments (code 32201) which employs 74 per cent of all workers in the industry and accounts for 65 per cent of its total sales. It is also the most heavily export-oriented, its exports accounting for 74 per cent of its sales in 1981. But it has the lowest value-added per worker of any sector (with the exception of the small domestically oriented sector producing "brassières and other undergarments"). "Spinning, weaving and finishing of textiles" which exports 64 per cent of its sales is the second largest sector, followed by "socks, briefs, singlets and other knitted wear" (45 per cent exported).

Table 52. Principal statistics of sectors of the textile and garments industry in Singapore, 1970-81

	1970	1975	1980	1981
Code 32111-2				
Spinning, weaving and finishing of textiles				
Number of establishments	15	29	39	36
Number of workers	3 324	6 160	5 653	4 760
Value added (S$m)	14.0	46.0	101.2	82.2
Value added per worker (S$'000)	4.2	7.5	17.9	17.3
Total sales (S$m)	54.4	161.4	265.5	235.3
Direct export as per cent of total sales (S$m)	57.3	60.5	58.9	63.6
Capital spending/employee remuneration	2.7	0.92	0.93	0.49
Code 32121				
Curtains, pillow cases, sheets and bedspreads				
Number of establishments	6	5	–	–
Number of workers	141	383	–	–
Value added (S$m)	0.2	1.8	–	–
Value added per worker (S$'000)	1.4	4.7	–	–
Total sales (S$m)	0.7	4.5	–	–
Direct export as per cent of total sales (S$m)	62.2	41.6	–	–
Capital spending/employee remuneration	4.1	0.14	–	–
Code 32131				
Knitted fabrics and laces				
Number of establishments	–	6	19	19
Number of workers	–	938	1 361	1 119
Value added (S$m)	–	6.0	26.1	27.2
Value added per worker (S$'000)	–	6.4	19.2	24.3
Total sales (S$m)	–	23.9	109.8	110.0
Direct export as per cent of total sales (S$m)	–	15.7	20.7	18.7
Capital spending/employee remuneration	–	2.68	0.23	0.32
Code 32132-3				
Socks, briefs, singlets and other knitted wear				
Number of establishments	16	17	26	22
Number of workers	2 519	2 797	2 135	1 416
Value added (S$m)	6.6	14.7	22.2	15.4
Value added per worker (S$'000)	2.6	5.2	10.4	10.8
Total sales (S$m)	17.0	37.3	63.3	38.4
Direct export as per cent of total sales (S$m)	31.7	60.4	67.8	45.2
Capital spending/employee remuneration	0.67	0.11	0.24	0.18
Code 32140-50				
Carpets, rugs, ropes, nets and related products				
Number of establishments	–	4	–	–
Number of workers	–	323	–	–
Value added (S$m)	–	2.5	–	–
Value added per worker (S$'000)	–	7.8	–	–
Total sales (S$m)	–	8.2	–	–
Direct export as per cent of total sales (S$m)	–	9.4	–	–
Capital spending/employee remuneration	–	0.04	–	–

Table 52.   *(continued)*

	1970	1975	1980	1981
Other textiles				
Number of establishments	12	11	15	17
Number of workers	1 067	779	561	611
Value added (S$m)	2.7	7.7	8.1	10.1
Value added per worker (S$'000)	2.5	9.9	14.5	16.5
Total sales (S$m)	9.6	22.2	36.9	36.6
Direct export as per cent of total sales (S$m)	40.4	67.1	43.8	33.1
Capital spending/employee remuneration	1.17	0.32	2.16	0.15
Code 32201 [1]				
Shirts				
Number of establishments	30	41	312	317
Number of workers	1 208	2 401	25 838	26 545
Value added (S$m)	4.1	15.0	251.6	291.8
Value added per worker (S$'000)	3.4	6.2	9.7	11.0
Total sales (S$m)	15.5	45.3	809.1	875.2
Direct export as per cent of total sales (S$m)	40.9	35.3	73.5	73.9
Capital spending/employee remuneration	0.26	0.23	0.22	0.20
Code 32202				
Other outer garments				
Number of establishments	69	136	–	–
Number of workers	7 439	14 034	–	–
Value added (S$m)	15.8	69.4	–	–
Value added per worker (S$'000)	2.1	4.9	–	–
Total sales (S$m)	59.9	219.7	–	–
Direct export as per cent of total sales (S$m)	78.9	81.5	–	–
Capital spending/employee remuneration	0.51	0.15	–	–
Code 32203-4				
Brassières and other undergarments				
Number of establishments	19	21	15	18
Number of workers	454	570	435	502
Value added (S$m)	1.0	2.5	4.6	6.5
Value added per worker (S$'000)	2.1	4.4	10.6	13.0
Total sales (S$m)	3.6	7.3	13.8	17.5
Direct export as per cent of total sales (S$m)	22.6	16.7	25.5	22.5
Capital spending/employee remuneration	0.30	0.12	0.41	0.27
Code 32205				
Tailoring and dressmaking				
Number of establishments	36	40	32	26
Number of workers	701	707	475	395
Value added (S$m)	2.5	3.9	5.8	5.3
Value added per worker (S$'000)	3.6	5.5	12.2	13.4
Total sales (S$m)	5.0	8.6	13.7	13.6
Direct export as per cent of total sales (S$m)	2.0	1.5	1.7	2.0
Capital spending/employee remuneration	0.01	0.14	0.35	0.12

Table 52. *(concl.)*

	1970	1975	1980	1981
Code 32209				
Other wearing apparel, except footwear				
Number of establishments	8	14	15	13
Number of workers	185	254	440	428
Value added (S$m)	0.4	1.3	4.4	4.7
Value added per worker (S$'000)	2.2	5.2	9.9	11.1
Total sales (S$m)	1.7	4.4	11.8	11.5
Direct export as per cent of total sales (S$m)	53.2	31.3	29.6	17.6
Capital spending/employee remuneration	0.08	0.25	0.52	0.11
Total				
Number of establishments	211	324	473	468
Number of workers	17 038	29 346	36 898	35 776
Value added (S$m)	47.3	170.8	424.0	443.2
Value added per worker (S$'000)	2.8	5.8	11.5	12.4
Total sales (S$m)	167.4	542.7	1 324.0	1 338.0
Direct export as per cent of total sales (S$m)	57.5	62.5	63.5	63.7
Capital spending/employee remuneration	1.10	0.45	0.40	0.25

[1] For 1980 and 1981, code 32201 includes other outer garments.

Sources: Singapore, Department of Statistics: *Report on the Census of Industrial Production, 1970* (Singapore, Government Printing Office, 1972), p. 37; idem: *Report on the Census of Industrial Production, 1975* (Singapore, Photoplates Private Ltd., 1976), pp. 43-44; idem: *Report on the Census of Industrial Production, 1980* (Singapore, Singapore National Printers, 1981), p. 67; idem: *Report on the Census of Industrial Production, 1981* (Singapore, Namic Printers Pte Ltd., 1982), p. 67.

Comparison of the electronics and textile and garments industries

The electronics, textile and garments industries in Singapore share many characteristics. Both began with a small number of local firms producing for the limited domestic market under import tariff protection. Then in the late 1960s both turned to export manufacturing and experienced explosive growth. Electronics production is dominated by offshore sourcing multinational companies, while textile and garments firms are mostly set up by Chinese businessmen from Hong Kong and elsewhere, many of whom have acquired Singapore permanent residence, and/or have local citizen partners.

Electronics is more heavily export-oriented than the textile and garments industry which still sells a third of its products locally. In the electronics industry, the multinational subsidiaries sell directly to their parent or sister companies, and to final customers, while local firms subcontract to the multinationals or to foreign buyers. Textile and garments manufacturers sell directly abroad to final customers, or subcontract to foreign buyers. Both industries are vulnerable to swings of the business cycle in importing countries, but electronics somewhat more so, as shown by its massive lay-offs during the world recession of 1975, and smaller lay-offs in 1981. Electronics is, however, more world-competitive than textiles and garments, which are protected by MFA quotas.

Both industries are labour-intensive, and together employ 40 per cent of all manufacturing workers in Singapore. Most of these workers – 90 per cent in electronics, 83 per cent in textile and garments – are women. Both depended on imported foreign labour in the early 1970s, until the electronics industry laid off and sent home most of its foreign workers during the 1975 recession. Today, about 10 per cent of electronics workers are foreigners, compared with 27 per cent of textile and garment workers. Textile and garment workers have lower skill and educational levels than electronics workers, perform more manual operations, and have less capital equipment to work with. Output and value-added per worker in textile and garments are less than half that in electronics. Wages in both industries are below the mean for manufacturing, the lowest-paid sector in Singapore. Average remuneration in electronics is about 20 per cent below the manufacturing average, while that in textile and garments is even lower.

Electronics is a technologically dynamic, rapidly growing world industry. The multinationals that dominate the Singapore industry are highly competitive, and quickly responsive to international market forces and to product and technology changes in the industry. They are not strongly influenced by government industrial policies, although they do benefit from the incentives offered. The textile and garments industry, however, is heavily dependent on policy interventions for its survival and progress. Domestic tariffs protection and preferential access to export markets through the MFA quotas enable the Singapore industry to compete despite its higher costs and declining comparative advantage. The easy importation of foreign workers also helps to keep costs lower than they would otherwise be. Whereas the electronics industry began upgrading during and after the 1975 recession, the textile and garments industry did not do so on a large scale until the Government instituted its three-year wage correction policy in 1979 and started using mechanisation and automation as additional criteria for allocating MFA quotas.

Unlike electronics, which is fast-growing and dynamic and vital to Singapore's restructuring strategy, textiles and garments is a slowly growing industry world-wide, beset by increasing supply-side competition and demand-side market constraints, such as greater protectionism and stagnating demand in importing countries. Singapore's comparative advantage in this industry is maintained only by extra-market interventions. Upgrading in the industry may slow the decline in its competitiveness and provide some insurance against increased protectionism or the loss of the MFA quotas. The long-term outlook for the textile sector is particularly bleak because of severe market competition and unavailability of labour. But that for the garments sector which has shown itself to be remarkably adaptable and resilient is slightly better. The sector has a growing reputation for quality and continues to benefit greatly from developed country importers who do not wish to become overly dependent on Hong Kong suppliers. Its major problem is that of the availability of labour: it is labour intensity that gives the sector its flexibility in responding to market changes quickly. Mechanisation and automation, the route taken by the textile industry, and the solution encouraged by government policy will reduce its flexibility. By 1991, should the Government stick to its announced policy of repatriating all foreign workers, the industry must shrink, even if external market conditions are favourable.

Notes

[1] For a detailed analysis of the electronics industry, see Pang Eng Fong and Linda Lim: *The electronics industry in Singapore – Structure, technology and linkages*, Economic Research Centre Monograph Series No. 7 (Singapore, University of Singapore, 1977); Linda Y. C. Lim: *Multinational firms and manufacturing for export in less-developed countries: The case of the electronics industry in Malaysia and Singapore*, Ph.D. dissertation, University of Michigan, 1978; and Linda Lim and Pang Eng Fong: *Technology choice and employment creation: A case study of three multinational enterprises in Singapore*, Multinational Enterprises Programme Working Paper No. 16 (Geneva, ILO, 1981).

[2] Economic Development Board: *Electronic firms in production in Singapore* (1983); and Science Council of Singapore and Association of Electronic Industries: *Singapore Electronics Buyers' Guide, 1980/81* (1982).

[3] Andrew Tanzer: "Asia plugs into the computer", in *Far Eastern Economic Review*, 21 July 1983.

[4] For reasons why employers prefer female workers in electronics assembly, see Linda Y. C. Lim: *Women workers in multinational corporations: The case of the electronics industry in Malaysia and Singapore*, Michigan Occasional Papers No. IX (Ann Arbor, Michigan, Fall 1978).

[5] Applied Research Corporation: "A study of electronics supporting industries" (Singapore, Aug. 1979; mimeographed).

[6] Pang Eng Fong and Augustine Tan: "Employment in the Singapore electronics industry", paper prepared for ILO Asian Regional Team for Employment Promotion (ARTEP) (Singapore, Apr. 1981), pp. 15-16.

[7] See Linda Y. C. Lim and Pang Eng Fong: "Vertical linkages and multinational enterprises in developing countries", in *World Development* (Oxford), July 1982, Vol. 10, No. 7, pp. 585-595.

[8] See Lim and Pang, *Technology choice . . .*, op. cit.

[9] See Lim and Pang, *Vertical linkages . . .*, op. cit.

Chapter 5

Lessons and prospects

The first three chapters provided a general account of Singapore's development experience since 1960. They paid particular attention to the institutional factors that underlie Singapore's ability to take advantage of favourable external conditions and build up its productive capacity. The fourth chapter related the particular experiences of two industries, namely electronics and textiles and garments, as examples of the contribution of public policy to industrial growth. In the concluding chapter we take a broad view of Singapore's development progress and analyse the internal and external factors that have contributed to the island's remarkable social and economic transformation and emergence as a newly industrialising country. We will separate the economic and non-economic factors that are unique to Singapore because of its history and geography from other factors that reflect the successful operation of social and economic policies. Our aim is to find out if there are lessons to be learnt from Singapore's development experience.

The importance of initial conditions

When Singapore began industrialising in 1960 it had a mixed colonial legacy. On the one hand, laissez-faire colonialism had made Singapore an efficient entrepot with good supporting services and infrastructure, and exposed its people to foreign goods and ideas. It had also created an English-speaking civil service that provided law and order but was not accustomed to regulating business closely. On the other hand, the colonial authorities had neglected the social and housing needs of an increasingly settled and rapidly growing population.

Apart from good infrastructure and an adaptable population, Singapore also enjoyed several initial advantages uncommon among developing countries. Firstly, it had an excellent harbour that needed no periodic dredging. Secondly, it was strategically located at the crossroads of seaborne trade between Asia and Europe. Thirdly, Singapore did not have a large backward agricultural sector, a sector that many developing countries have found hard to transform. Fourthly, its compactness as a city-State made it fairly easy for the Government to execute economic and social policies, the results of which were readily visible to the population. Thus effective government policies expanded political support which in turn ensured the success of subsequent policies.

If Singapore had some initial advantages, it also faced severe constraints when it embarked on a planned industrialisation programme in 1960. Firstly, as a small, compact island State, it lacked natural resources. Secondly, its domestic market was too small to support many viable industries. (Its small size in fact turned out later to be an advantage because it compelled Singapore to look to export markets after the loss of the Malaysian market in 1965 when Singapore withdrew from Malaysia.) Thirdly, the island, having depended largely on entrepot earnings for its prosperity, had no industrial tradition or reservoir of industrial skills. This constraint, like the small market limitation, was overcome by the adoption of a strategy that relied on the development of export markets by foreign companies which brought with them not only capital but also technology and expertise.

Singapore's initial conditions would have mattered little had the Government not adopted pragmatism as its guiding philosophy and instituted measures to ensure an efficient government and a healthy investment climate. Entrepot facilities would have deteriorated had the Government pursued an inward-looking strategy, as has happened, for example, with the once great port of Aden. In Singapore, contrary to its fiery socialist rhetoric, the ruling party when it came to power did not attempt to nationalise industries or restrict private enterprise and thus entrepreneurial activities. Had it done so, it would have created a large corps of regulators while discouraging the inflow of investors. Singapore's strategic location and fine harbour would have been bypassed by shippers and traders. In addition, the island's adaptable and outward-looking population would not have been as energetic and enterprising as it proved to be had the Government after 1959 abandoned the colonial commitment to free trade policies. In short, the island's initial advantages could have all disappeared had the Government not developed a pragmatic mix of economic and social policies to capitalise on favourable external conditions in the world economy.

It is misleading to think that initial conditions are unalterable and that they predetermine a country's development potential. In Singapore's case its geography was a given fact, so also were its lack of resources and the absence of an agricultural sector. But other and perhaps more important initial conditions such as the energy and enterprise of its people, and the openness of its economy were themselves the result of policies, in particular free trade policies that encourage risk-taking and receptiveness to new ideas. Other countries could also introduce policies to stimulate risk-taking behaviour and expose their people to new ideas and new ways of doing things.

Explaining Singapore's success story

Favourable world developments contributed to Singapore's rapid emergence as a newly industrialising country. But these developments would have been missed had Singapore not pursued an extraordinary blend of state intervention and economic liberalism. While applauding competition, the Singapore Government is not ideologically against intervention in various markets when such intervention is necessary for social stability or economic efficiency. For example, the Government acted early to build low-cost housing to give people a stake in Singapore and to keep down the costs of urban living. Beginning in the early 1970s it intervened in the labour market to ensure orderly wage changes so that Singapore could remain competitive in exporting labour-intensive goods. Since 1979, although the policy of keeping wages low has been replaced by one emphasising productivity and market-clearing wages, state intervention in the labour market through the mechanism of the tripartite NWC has not been abandoned. The Government also does not see public enterprises as inconsistent with its support of a free enterprise system. In the 1960s it started many public enterprises in industries that the private sector was unwilling to invest in. All the public enterprises were run on a profit basis with professional management. None has been allowed to be a drain on the public purse.

Besides intervening in the labour market, the State affects urban redevelopment through its land sales programme, regulates financial markets through its quasi-central bank, the MAS, and influences investment activities and resource allocation with various investment incentives. Despite the relative lack of controls on private production decisions and the dominance of market forces because of its open economy, Singapore's domestic economy is far from a laissez-faire one. Its success is not, as some observers have suggested, testimony to the "magic of the marketplace" but rather to the shrewd, flexible, pragmatic use of interventionist policies and market signals to accelerate economic growth while satisfying basic needs and providing a high level of public services. From the start the Government viewed its intervention in the economy from the objective of expanding industrial capacity and improving economic performance. While it provided low-cost housing, education and medical services, it did not confuse the goal of economic efficiency in production with the goal of equity in distribution.

Some analysts suggest that strong governmental leadership would not be possible if Singapore with its largely Chinese population were not a Confucianist society. They argue that Confucianist values such as respect for authority, loyalty to good leaders, preference for order and harmony, and a taste for hard work and accumulation contribute greatly to Singapore's success. Their cultural explanation, however, is based on a selective interpretation of Confucianism. Historically, Confucianism provided a set of ideals and guides for political life. It emphasised obedience to benevolent rulers as its central value and loyalty to rulers as an extension of family loyalty. After the emergence of four economically dynamic Confucianist-influenced societies, namely those of Japan, the Republic of Korea, Hong Kong and Singapore, it was seen by many as a doctrine to preserve traditional order rather than to promote economic and social progress. In Singapore many institutions with their stress on strong and orderly administration are Confucianist in character. But to say that Confucianism is a key factor in Singapore's success is to stretch the explanatory power of culture and to slight the importance of flexible, pragmatic economic policies.

Lessons from Singapore's experience

Without comparative data it is difficult to say whether Singapore's unique blend of state leadership and economic freedom is right also for other countries. It would be rash to suggest that the Singapore path to development is the only one; many other countries including Brazil and the Republic of Korea using different mixes of market signals and planning have also succeeded in their industrialisation efforts. Nevertheless, we believe there are a number of lessons that could be learned from Singapore's experience in rapid industrialisation. Firstly, Singapore's experience underscores the importance of flexibility in institutions and policies in adjusting to changing internal and external conditions. In the early 1960s the island went through a short but mild phase of import-substituting industrialisation, but the Government moved away from this strategy to emphasise labour-intensive manufacturing exports after 1965 when the enlarged domestic market failed to materialise. In the late 1970s, because of growing competition from other producers of labour-intensive exports, rising protectionism in industrial countries and domestic labour shortages, it began promoting high-value activities by providing support – training grants, investment incentives, improved infrastructure – to encourage firms to introduce new technologies and individuals to learn new skills.

Secondly, the Government did not introduce for reasons of nationalism or distributional equity price distortions into the economic system. Even during its brief period of import-substituting industrialisation, it did not make extensive use of direct measures such as licenses, quotas, price controls to influence private decision-making. Consequently, efficient resource allocation was encouraged because both producers and consumers responded to price signals from world markets. Because the Government avoided direct measures, interest groups dependent on licenses did not grow and entrench themselves. There was also less scope for arbitrary and self-seeking decision-making by public officials.

Thirdly, from the beginning the Government realised the importance of an attractive investment climate. Accordingly, it not only introduced suitable investment incentives but also measures to ensure industrial peace and wage stability. It ensured a co-operative labour union movement by various legal and political means. In the 1960s relative wage stability was assured by excess labour supply and in the 1970s by the importation of foreign workers and effective wage guide-lines. As a result, throughout the 1960s and 1970s real wages grew more slowly than the rate of economic growth. The lesson from Singapore's experience is that a government must act firmly to ensure wage stability and industrial peace. It must strike the right balance between rising wage demands in growing industries during the early stages of industrialisation and the need to create jobs and keep the growth momentum going.

A fourth lesson from Singapore's experience is that a country can benefit from foreign ideas and technology without compromising its economic and political sovereignty. From the start, the Singapore Government realised the importance of foreign capital and technology to its development. It has not tried to limit the participation of foreign firms in most sectors of the economy. However, it makes abundantly clear to foreign investors that they are not free to pursue actions contrary to Singapore's national interests or involve themselves in domestic politics. It earns the respect of foreign firms by dealing with them in a businesslike manner, avoiding arbitrary, capricious actions that might upset their planning. Unlike the governments of many inward-looking countries, the Singapore Government did not view foreign firms as a threat to its sovereignty but as essential to the country's stability and prosperity.

Yet another lesson that Singapore offers is the importance of measures to mobilise domestic savings and sound public finance. Throughout two decades of rapid growth the Government practised financial conservatism, tightly controlling public spending on non-development-related items. As a result, each year the Government enjoyed public sector surpluses in its current account. For development spending the Government relied mainly on domestic savings mobilised through the CPF, a workers' retirement scheme to which both employees and employers must contribute. It did not depend on deficit financing or foreign aid for public sector development programmes. Public sector surpluses and a high rate of forced savings which had a deflationary effect on the economy helped to keep Singapore's inflation rate below the average for the world.

In general, the chief lesson of Singapore's development experience for other countries is that an efficient, honest and forward-looking state apparatus, unencumbered by doctrinaire political or economic philosophy, and ever-responsive to changes in market forces, can effectively mobilise a country's people and resources to make the most of those prevailing market forces. Popular support for the development effort is crucial, and is obtained by ensuring that the basic needs of the population are quickly met, by the State if necessary.

Development policies and prospects for the 1980s

For the past 20-odd years, the performance of the Singapore economy with respect to growth, price stability, employment and improvement in real living standards has been one of the best in the world. This economic success has been the result of both favourable market forces and government development strategy.

Towards the end of the 1970s changes in domestic and international market forces prompted changes in government development policy. In particular, Singapore is gradually losing its comparative advantage in the export of labour-intensive manufactures – a key sector of the economy in the 1960s and 1970s – because of domestic labour shortages, rising wages, an appreciating exchange rate, increased supply-side competition from other newly industrialising and developing countries, and the demand-side constraints of slow growth and increased protectionism in developed country markets.

For the 1980s the Government has set a growth target of 8-10 per cent a year, in order to reach by 1990 Japanese per capita GNP in 1980. This target requires annual productivity increases of 6-8 per cent, double the average rates achieved during the 1970s. Manufacturing is to remain the prime mover of the economy, increasing its share of GDP from 23 per cent in 1980 to 31 per cent in

1990. Trade, tourism, transport and communications, and "brain services" are also projected to grow rapidly.[1]

Development strategy for the 1980s is to restructure the economy, especially the manufacturing sector, from its present low-wage, labour-intensive base, into higher-productivity, higher-technology, more capital-intensive and "upmarket" activities. The recently abandoned wage correction policy was a first step in this direction; it aimed at stimulating the phasing out or upgrading of labour-intensive activities. More generous tax and other incentives are being offered to high-value, high-productivity manufacturing investments. And the Government has embarked on an accelerated skilled manpower training programme through its various tertiary and technical training institutes.

Foreign capital, enterprise, technology and expertise will be even more vigorously encouraged than previously, given the lack of an indigenous capacity and comparative advantage in high-technology activities. More foreign skilled and professional personnel will be encouraged not only to work, but also to settle permanently in Singapore, and more foreign students will be admitted into Singapore's educational and training institutes to make up the shortfall of available citizen school-leavers for the planned manpower training programmes. Until 1991 foreign labour from "traditional" sources (Malaysia, Hong Kong, the Republic of Korea) will be allowed into the country on short-term contracts to alleviate labour shortages, especially in the construction sector. Foreign labour from non-traditional sources will be phased out by 1986.

Economic liberalisation in the form of the removal of protection for goods and services will accelerate. Many of the various remaining controls on foreign participation in traded and untraded services will be changed, making these sectors as open to competition as manufacturing.

At the same time the Government is undertaking a major campaign to increase productivity, and has set up a tripartite council for this purpose. A keystone of the campaign is emulation of several aspects of the Japanese industrial relations and management system. There will be increased "privatisation" of social benefits to encourage workers to identify closely with the employers.

Much of Singapore's economic and social success to date, and the profitability of private business operating in the country, have been based on the State's responsibility for workers' welfare. The Government provides subsidised housing, health, educational and recreational services for the mass of the population, and manages the bulk of savings for retirement through the CPF. It also influences annual wage increments and sets minimum fringe benefits. This role of government has won it the support and dependence of the population, and also minimised company responsibility for worker welfare.

The Government has now proposed that employers be allowed to use part of their contributions to the CPF to provide more employee benefits. It is encouraging company welfare schemes for employees for two reasons. First, it appears increasingly unwilling to provide subsidised social services – particularly housing and medical care – to match the ever-increasing demand and expectations of the population because of ever-rising costs and its aversion to subsidies and preference for market-based pricing. Second, it feels that dependence of workers on the State has prevented the development of company loyalty which it believes is conducive to employment stability and skill upgrading.

The prospects for Singapore's achievement of the Government's desired growth and productivity targets, a restructured economy and social order depend, as in the past, on both external and internal factors. Externally, the success of industrial upgrading depends heavily on world demand and supply conditions, particularly on competition from other newly industrialising countries, on growth of the world economy and market access to developed countries, and on the availability to Singapore of technical and professional manpower essential to high-technology manufacturing but which is in such short supply all over the world today.

Internally, the success of the "privatisation" strategy depends on the extent to which it is accepted by both companies and workers – neither of whom will be happy if they stand to lose anything from the change. For example, companies may not be willing to bear the additional expense of responsibility for worker welfare, while workers may be reluctant to forgo the security and relative equity of State-provided social benefits.

"Privatisation" does not necessarily mean more laissez-faire. The Government will continue to decide on economic policy and will retain its social and political control of the population despite their decreasing dependence on the State. In the labour market stronger company-worker ties may reduce the flexibility of employers and the mobility of workers in adjusting to changing market forces, thereby making less efficient than now resource allocation in Singapore's open economy. Privatisation may also increase inflationary pressures and widen real income disparities in the economy.

Although the Singapore Government may seem to have moved sharply from the left to the right of the political spectrum since self-government in 1959, its original socialist philosophy – employment creation as the primary goal of development under state direction, and state responsibility for many basic needs and social welfare – in fact laid the political, social and economic foundations for the current shift towards a more laissez-faire economy. Its singular achievement in nearly a quarter-century of unbroken rule is the way it has delicately balanced the benefits of social controls and economic freedoms with their costs. State-provided social benefits protect the population against the inherent insecurities of the market while market competition constrains the power the State wields over the population through its provision of social benefits. As the State shifts more of the burden of providing social benefits to private employers, the population's vulnerability to economic fluctuations will increase.

While the Government's role in the provision of social benefits may diminish in the future, its interventions in the social sphere will likely expand. The Government considers social controls and campaigns essential for social harmony and political stability. Without stability, the Government believes, international confidence in Singapore will evaporate quickly. So long as social peace and economic growth prevail, and they seem likely to do so for the rest of the 1980s, the population will continue to accept the Government-defined need for extensive social interventions.

Note

[1] For details, see "Highlights of Singapore's economic development plan for the eighties", Appendix I of *Towards higher achievement*, Budget Speech 1981, by Goh Chok Tong, Minister for Trade and Industry (March 1981).